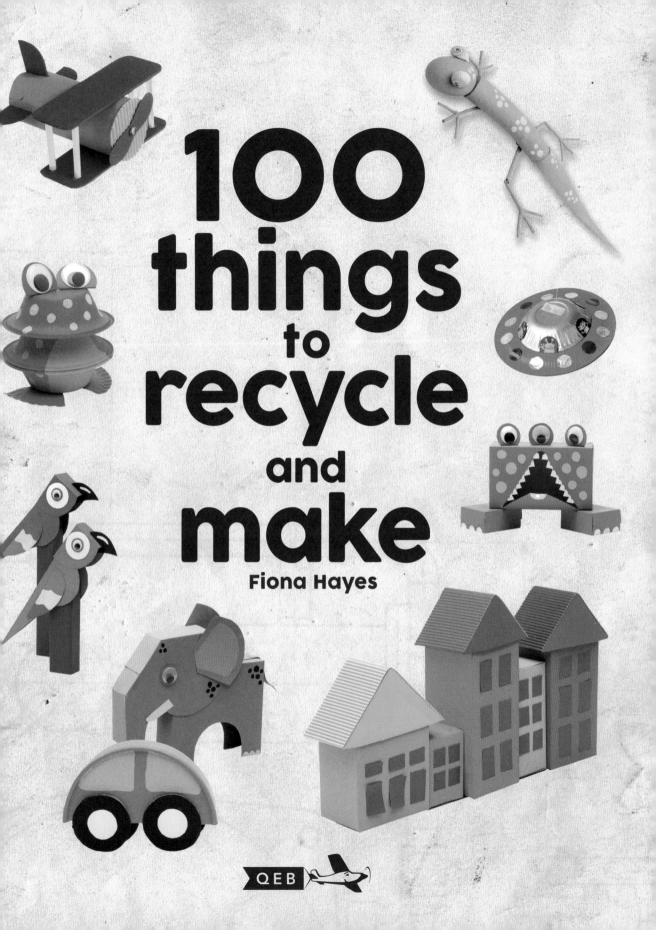

100
things
to
recycle
and
make

Fiona Hayes

QEB

Basic Equipment

Most of these projects use some or all of the following equipment, so keep these handy:

- **White glue**
- **Scissors**
- **Pencils**
- **Ruler**
- **Felt-tip pens**
- **Paintbrushes**

Contents

CARDBOARD BOXES

PAPER PLATES

CARDBOARD TUBES

NATURE CRAFT

EGG CARTONS

Giraffe

This gorgeous giraffe will look great in your bedroom. Why not make two and use them as bookends?

You will need

Two cereal boxes

Three long boxes

Brown, yellow, pink, and green paint

Brown cardboard

Thin cardstock

Two googly eyes

One yellow straw

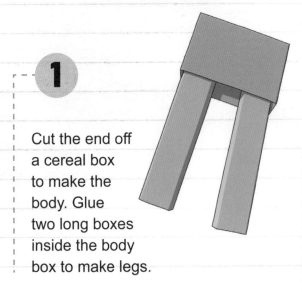

1

Cut the end off a cereal box to make the body. Glue two long boxes inside the body box to make legs.

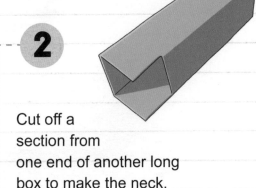

2

Cut off a section from one end of another long box to make the neck.

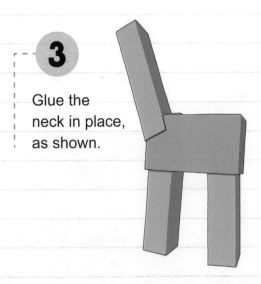

3

Glue the neck in place, as shown.

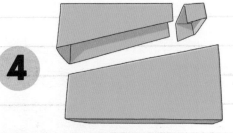

4

Cut a wedge from another cereal box, as shown. This top part will be the head. Recycle the rest of the box.

5

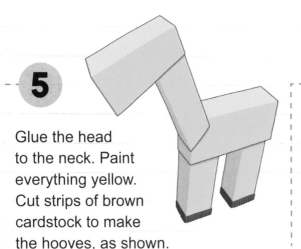

Glue the head to the neck. Paint everything yellow. Cut strips of brown cardstock to make the hooves, as shown.

6

Cut out a pair of ears from cardstock, paint them yellow, and glue them in place. Paint on lots of brown spots.

7

Cut a rectangle of brown cardboard to cover the snout. Then cut a strip to make the mane and some for the tail. Cut circles of thin cardstock and paint green. Glue the eyes to the green circles and fix to the head. Cut two short pieces of straw for horns. Paint details such as a smile. Add pink to the ears to finish your giraffe.

Handy Hint

For stand-out eyes, cut circles slightly bigger than the googly eyes. Paint them a bright color and glue the eyes to the circles.

Crane

Building sites are busy, busy, busy! Can you build a crane to help lift the heavy loads?

You will need

Small cereal box	Eight bottle tops
Paint	Cardstock
Three narrow boxes	Two bendy straws
Corrugated cardstock	

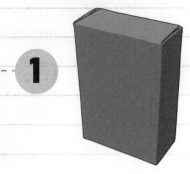

1 Paint a small cereal box.

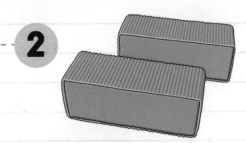

2 Paint two narrow boxes in a different color. Glue a strip of corrugated cardstock around four edges of each box, as shown.

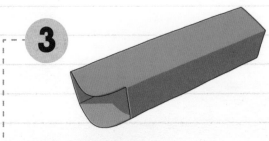

3 Cut the end of another narrow box, as shown. Paint it to match the other boxes in step 2.

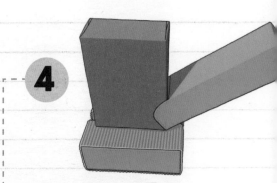

4 Glue the narrow boxes to the blue box, as shown.

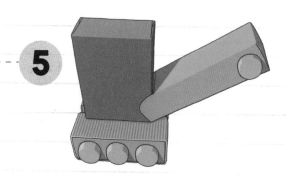

5 Glue on the bottle tops for the track rollers and the crane winch.

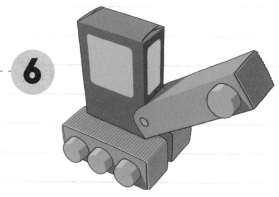

6 Cut out some windows from cardstock and glue onto the cab. Add a dot of paint for the screw on the winch.

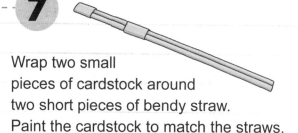

7 Wrap two small pieces of cardstock around two short pieces of bendy straw. Paint the cardstock to match the straws.

8 Make a hole in the base of the crane arm with the tip of a pencil. Glue the straws in place to make the crane grab. Get ready, steady, build!

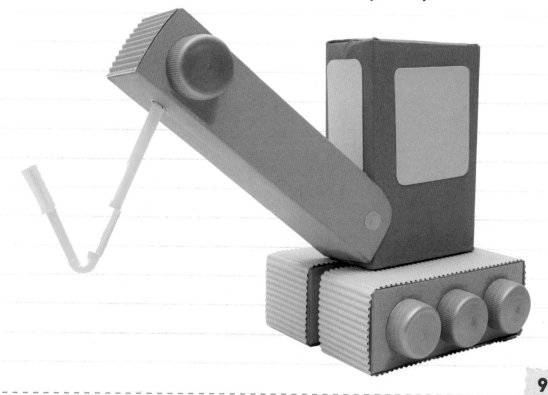

Parrot

Who's a clever bird, then?
This parrot and its friend!
Make these jungle birds and
put them in your bedroom.

1

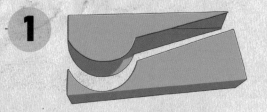

For each parrot, cut the side
of a box as shown. You need
the top part for the parrot's body.

2

 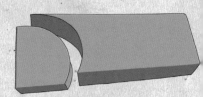

Cut a curved corner off
another box to make
the parrot's head.

3

Paint the pieces and
glue them together.

4

Cut out a beak from cardboard
and paint it black.

5

Cut a slit in the front of the head,
slide in the beak, and glue to hold.

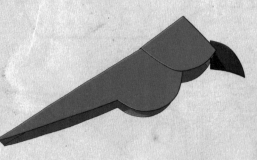

6

Cut out a pair of wings from cardboard and paint feathers, as shown.

7

Glue on the wings. Cut out two circles from the cardstock and glue them to either side of the head. Glue on a pair of googly eyes, as shown.

8

Paint around the eyes and add detail to the beak. Paint the narrow box brown. Glue the box into the middle of the body so the parrot has a perch. Repeat all the steps to make the second parrot— why not paint it in different colors?

Handy Hint

Cut the perches at different heights so the birds look like they are on different trees.

Tiger

Grrrr! Tigers are stripy, orange, and fluffy. But, beware, these cats are anything but cute!

1

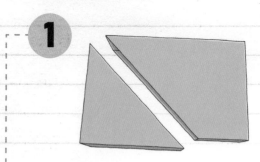

Cut the corner off a cereal box.

2

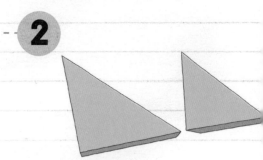

Cut another smaller corner out of the cereal box.

3

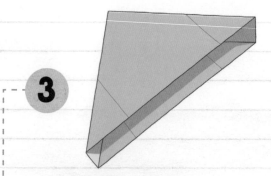

Cut four slits in the larger triangle, as shown. This will be the tiger's body.

4

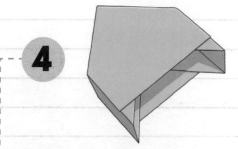

Fold the ends into the middle and glue to hold in place so you have a shape that looks like a house. Cut off any parts that stick out from the bottom so you have a flat base.

5

Glue the smaller triangle on top of the bigger one. Paint the tiger orange with a white tummy and muzzle.

6

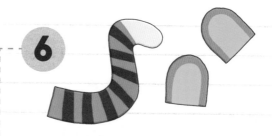

Cut out a tail and a pair of ears from cardstock. Paint them as shown.

7

Glue the ears and tail in place. Paint black stripes onto the tiger's body.

GRRR
GRRR

8

Glue on a pair of googly eyes and a bottle top for the nose. Add a mouth to finish off your tiger. Now, your tiger is ready to roar!

Flamingo

What's bright pink, feathery, and lives in Africa? A flamingo!

You will need

One cereal box

Two long boxes

One small box

Cardstock

Pink, white, black, and yellow paint

Two googly eyes

1

Cut the corner off a large cereal box.

2

Cut another triangular section from the rest of the box. Use the corner you cut in step 1 as a template.

3

Slide one section into the other to make a closed triangle for the body. Glue in place and paint pink.

4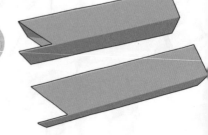

Cut out a triangular section from the end of each long box. These will be the neck and legs.

5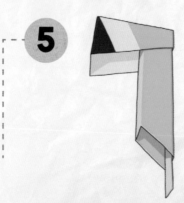

Cut the end off a smaller box to make a head. Glue the neck box in place. Paint the neck and part of the head pink. Give the flamingo a white and black beak.

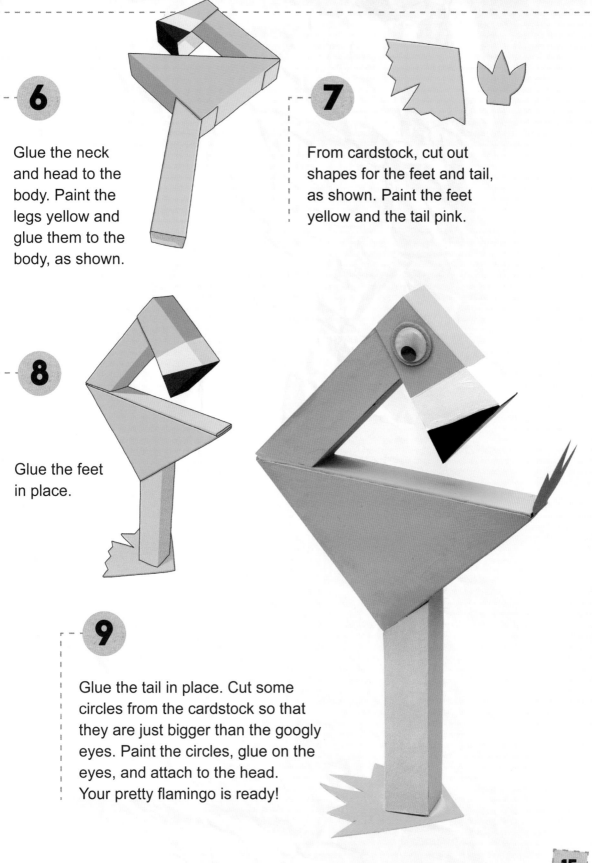

6

Glue the neck and head to the body. Paint the legs yellow and glue them to the body, as shown.

7

From cardstock, cut out shapes for the feet and tail, as shown. Paint the feet yellow and the tail pink.

8

Glue the feet in place.

9

Glue the tail in place. Cut some circles from the cardstock so that they are just bigger than the googly eyes. Paint the circles, glue on the eyes, and attach to the head. Your pretty flamingo is ready!

Beetle Cars

Beep! Beep! It's time to take these beetle cars for a drive.

You will need

One round box

Paint, including black, blue, and white

Cardboard

1 Glue the lid of the round box to the box base. Cut the box in half to make two car bodies.

2 Cut out four circles from cardboard. Paint them to look like wheels.

3 Paint the body of each car. When dry, paint two windows on either side.

4 Glue the wheels in place. Vroom, vroom! These little cars make great toys for rainy days!

Tulips

Tulips are beautiful, brightly colored flowers. Why not make a bunch of these pretty blooms and put them in a vase?

You will need

Two round boxes

Paint

Four green straws

1

To make two tulips, glue the lid to the base of the round box. Cut it in half.

2

Cut out small triangles to give each half a zig-zag edge.

3

Paint your tulips different colors. Paint the insides too.

4

Use a pencil to make a hole in the bottom of each tulip. Glue a straw into each hole for a stem.

5

Repeat steps 1 to 4 with the second box to make two more tulips. They will make a lovely gift for someone special.

Birdhouse Bank

Count your pennies and save all your money in this colorful birdhouse.

You will need

Tall box
Paint
Cardboard
One straw

1

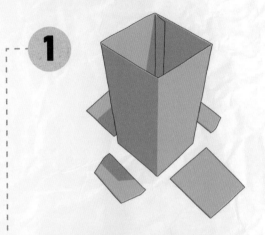

Cut the top flaps off a tall box.

2

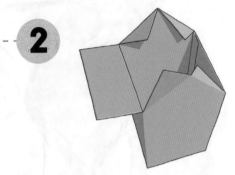

Cut slits in each corner. Fold in the edges to make a triangle at the front and back.

3

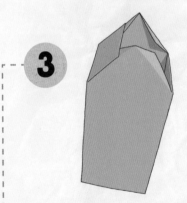

Glue one of the rectangular flaps to the edge of the triangle, as shown. Cut off the other flap.

4

Use a pencil to start a hole for your scissors. Cut out an entrance hole, as shown. Paint the box a bright, pretty color.

5

Cut a rectangle of cardboard and fold it in half to make the roof. Paint it a contrasting color to the birdhouse.

6

Glue one side of the roof to the top of the box. Leave the other side so you can open the box to get your money.

7

Make a hole with a pencil in the front of the box. Glue in a piece of straw for a perch. Now you can start saving your money for something special!

Handy Hint

Make sure the entrance hole in your birdhouse is bigger than your biggest coin.

Big Mouth Monster

This monster has a BIG MOUTH. Make your monster scary or funny—you decide!

1

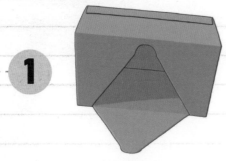

You need a box with an opening flap on it. Paint it a bright color on the outside and a different color on the inside.

2

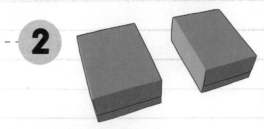

Paint two matchboxes. These will be the feet.

3

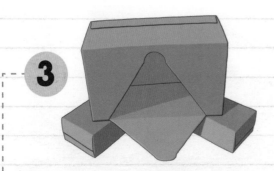

Glue the monster's body to the feet. Make sure the flap is at the front.

4

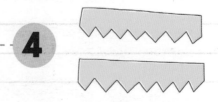

Cut two narrow strips of white cardstock. Then cut out triangles along one edge of the strips. These will be the teeth.

5

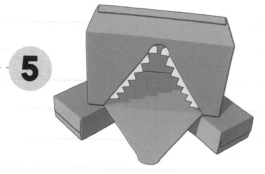

Glue the teeth to the inside
of the top of the mouth, as shown.

6

Cut three circles
from cardstock. They
should be slightly
bigger than the
googly eyes. Paint the circles
the same color as the body,
and glue on the eyes.

7

Glue the eyes to the top of the box.
Paint on some spots and toenails. Your
monster is ready to scare your friends!

ARRR

Elephant

Elephants live in a herd so why don't you make your elephant a friend?

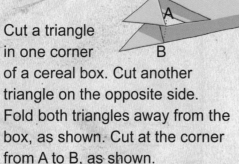

1 Cut a triangle in one corner of a cereal box. Cut another triangle on the opposite side. Fold both triangles away from the box, as shown. Cut at the corner from A to B, as shown.

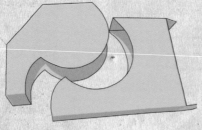

2 Fold the triangles and flaps into the box. Glue to hold in place.

3 Cut out a head shape from the box, as shown.

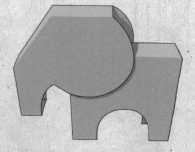

4 Cut out a semicircle from another box to make the body.

5 Paint both boxes gray. Glue the head to the body.

Handy Hint

If you cut the wrong part in step 1, do not worry—you can always tape it back together.

6

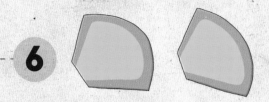

Cut out a pair of ears from cardstock. Paint them gray with pink in the middle.

7

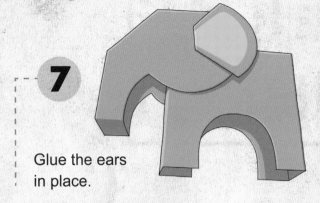

Glue the ears in place.

8

Cut out a tail and pair of tusks from the cardstock. Paint the tail gray. Cut out purple circles and glue the eyes to them. Glue on the tail, tusks, and eyes. Paint on some spots and toenails to finish your elephant.

CUTE

Pirate Ship

Arrggh! Calling all pirates! Prepare to set sail on the seven seas in this pirate ship.

1

Carefully open the ends of a large cereal box. Cut off the flaps, as shown.

2

Cut a slit down one edge and fold back the side at an angle. Repeat on all four of the base corners.

3

Fold the corners in and bring the base and top sides together. Glue to hold in place. This will give you a ship-shaped base.

4

Paint the shaped box brown.

5

Paint two different sized boxes brown and glue them to the large box, as shown.

6

Cut out lots of circles of cardstock and paint as portholes. Glue them to the sides.

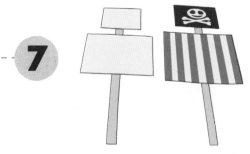

7

Cut out some sails from cardstock and paint them. Cut out some narrow strips of cardboard for the masts and paint yellow. Glue the sails to the masts.

8

Fold a piece of gray cardstock in half and cut out an anchor. Glue the anchor to the ship.

9

Make slits in the top box with a pencil and glue in the masts. Your pirate ship is ready to sail—arrggh, me hearties, land ahoy!

Handy Hint

Why not design your own flag to fly on your pirate ship?

Penguin

You will need

Chocolate box
Black and blue paint
Cardboard
White and yellow cardstock
Two googly eyes

1

Paint the box black.

2

Cut out a pair of wings from cardboard and paint them black.

3

Next, cut out a dome shape from white cardstock for the penguin's tummy.

4

Glue the wings and tummy in place.

5

Cut out two circles from the white cardstock. Paint them blue and glue the eyes to them. Glue the eyes in place.

6

Cut out a beak from yellow cardstock and glue it under the eyes. Your penguin is ready to swim.

Row of Houses Desk Bins

You will need

Eight cardboard boxes

Paint

Corrugated cardstock

Cardboard

1

You will need two boxes the same size for each house. To make each house, cut off the corner of one of the boxes, for the roof.

2

Fold the top flaps inside and glue to hold in place. This will make it stronger when you take the roof on and off. Paint the house.

3

Glue some corrugated cardstock to the roof and paint it.

4

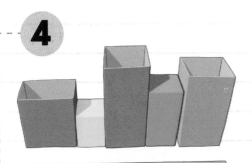

Now repeat steps 1 to 3 with the other boxes, but have some solid boxes, with closed tops, between the open ones. Glue the row of houses onto a strip of cardboard.

5

Put the roofs on the open-ended boxes. Cut out rectangles for windows and glue them to your houses. Put all your pens and pencils in the houses to keep your desk neat and tidy.

Ladybug Box

You will need

One round box

Cardboard

Black, red, and blue paint

Two googly eyes

Two metal fasteners

1

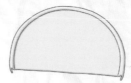

Cut the lid from the round box into slightly less than half. Recycle the bigger piece. Paint the smaller piece and the base of the box black.

2

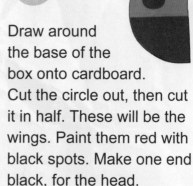

Draw around the base of the box onto cardboard. Cut the circle out, then cut it in half. These will be the wings. Paint them red with black spots. Make one end black, for the head.

3

Make a hole with the tip of a pencil through the wing and the lid section. Use a metal fastener to attach together. Repeat with the other wing.

4

Glue the lid to the base, but do not get any glue on the wings.

5

From cardboard, cut out circles that are slightly bigger than the eyes. Paint them blue and glue on a pair of googly eyes. Cut six legs from cardboard and paint black. Glue the eyes and legs to the ladybug.

Crown

This crown is fit for a Queen...or a King!

You will need

One cereal box

Paint, including yellow and gold

Cardstock

Glitter

1

Gently flatten a cereal box and cut it in half.

2

Cut out a row of triangles around one edge of the top half.

3

Paint your crown yellow.

4

Cut a strip of cardstock to fit around the bottom of the crown. Paint it gold and glue it in place.

5

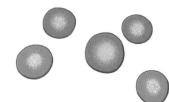

Cut out some circles from cardstock and paint them jewel-like colors. Add some glitter to the centers.

6

Glue the jewels to the tips of the crown and it will be fit for royalty!

29

Picnic Basket

You will need

One shoebox with a detachable lid

Paint, including green

Cardboard

1

Cut two slits in either side of the shoebox lid.

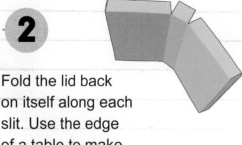

2

Fold the lid back on itself along each slit. Use the edge of a table to make a straight crease.

3

Paint the lid and the base of the box green. Paint some flowers on the base.

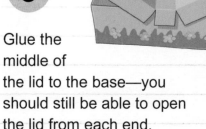

4

Cut and fold a strip of cardboard to make a handle. Make sure that it fits over the lid of the box.

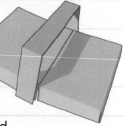

5

Glue the middle of the lid to the base—you should still be able to open the lid from each end.

6

Decorate the lid and glue the handle in place. Happy picnicking!

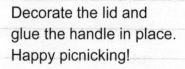

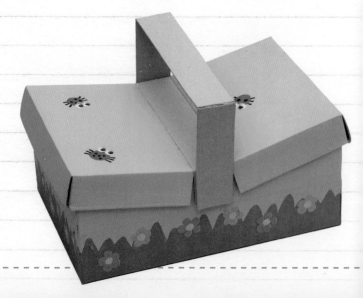

Whale

You'll have a whale of a time making this beautiful sea giant!

You will need

One shoebox with a detachable lid

Paint

One cardboard box

Cardstock

Two googly eyes

Paint the base of the shoebox dark blue on the outside and pink on the inside. Cut the end of the base diagonally, as shown.

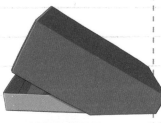

Paint the lid pale blue on the outside and pink on the inside. Glue the base to the lid so that it is open, as shown.

Cut out a heart-shaped corner from the other box. This will be the tail.

Paint the tail dark blue and glue it to the body.

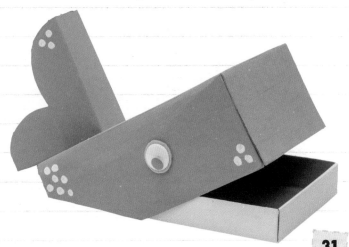

Cut out some circles of cardstock. Paint a contrasting color. Glue the eyes to the circles and attach to the whale's head. Paint on some spots to finish your whale.

Fish Tank

If you've always
wanted a fish tank,
make this fun and
colorful water world!

You will need

Rectangular tissue box

**Paint, including blue
and green**

Cardboard

Five googly eyes

Five blue bendy straws

1 Cut a large, rectangular hole
in the front of the tissue box.
Paint the inside of the box a
light blue and the outside of
the box a different shade of
blue. This is your fish tank.

2 On cardboard, draw a
triangle with a smaller
triangle overlapping it,
as shown. Then cut it out.
This will be one of your fish.

3 Use the template from
step 2 to cut out four
more fish. Paint the fish
bright colors. Glue an
eye on to each fish.

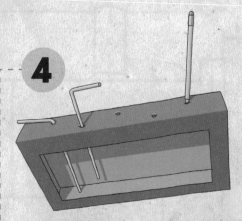

4 Use a pencil to make five
holes in the top of your
fish tank. Push a bendy
straw through each hole,
with the bend at the top.

5

Glue your fish to the
straws. Glue them at
different heights and
facing different directions.

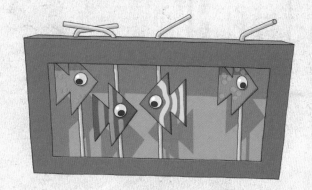

6

To make seaweed, cut out some wavy
pieces of cardboard and paint them
green. Glue them to the inside of the tank.
Twist the straws to make your fish swim.

GLUB
GLUB

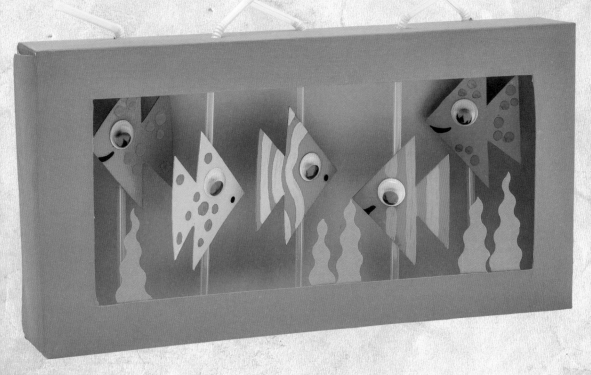

Robot

Make an army of
super-cool robots
to take over the
world! (Or just
your house.)

1

Paint two different
sized boxes. Then
glue the smaller
box to the top of
the larger box.

2

Glue two cardboard
tubes covered
with corrugated
cardstock to the
base of the large
box for legs.

3

Next, paint two
matchboxes and
glue them to
the cardboard
tubes. These
will be the feet.

4

To make each arm, cut the end
off a candy tube and paint it.
Cut out two circles of cardstock
and paint them. Use a metal
fastener to attach the open end
of the arms to the circles of
colored cardstock.

5

Glue the arms to either side of the body, as shown. You will be able to move the arms up and down.

6

Use the end of a pencil to make two holes at the top of the head. Insert two small pieces of bendy straw. Cut a rectangle of shiny paper for the front and glue in place.

7

Glue on some bottle tops for the eyes and ears. Add some googly eyes to the inside of the bottle tops and a strip of painted corrugated cardstock for a mouth.

8

Glue some tube tops and colored cardstock circles to the robot's tummy to decorate it. Your robot is complete—have lots of fun playing with it!

Cool Cat

1

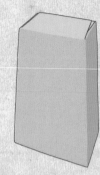

Paint the box yellow.

2

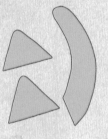

Cut out a pair of ears and a tail from cardboard and paint them yellow.

3

Paint the middle of the ears pink. Glue them and the tail in place.

4

Cut out a dome shape from white cardstock for the cat's tummy. Glue it to the front of the box. Paint some stripes onto the rest of the box.

5

Cut out a semicircle of pink felt for the cat's nose. Glue the nose and a pair of eyes to the face. Draw on a mouth. If you have some smaller boxes, you can make some cute kittens.

Stegosaurus

This large, armored dinosaur is a plant-eating friendly giant! Can you make any more dinos?

You will need

One paper plate
Paint
Cardboard
One googly eye

1 For the body, cut the bottom off a paper plate and paint it.

2 Cut out a head, tail, and a pair of legs from cardboard. Paint them a contrasting color to the body.

3 Glue the head, tail, and legs to the back of the plate.

4 Cut out some triangles from cardboard and paint them. Glue them along the top of the body.

5 Paint on lots of spots, including one for the eye, and a mouth. Glue on a googly eye. Your dinosaur is ready to stomp!

37

Flower Hat

You'll look great in this pretty flower hat!

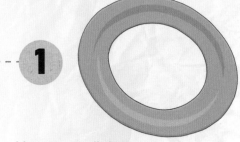

You will need

One paper plate
One paper bowl
Paint, including yellow
Cardstock
Tissue paper
Ribbon

1

Use a pencil tip to make a hole for your scissors and cut out the middle of a paper plate.

2

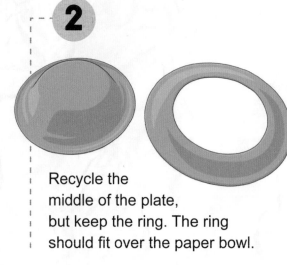

Recycle the middle of the plate, but keep the ring. The ring should fit over the paper bowl.

3

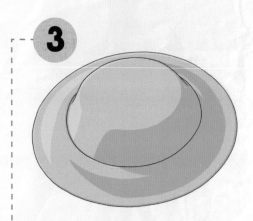

Place the ring over the paper bowl. Glue to hold in place. Paint your hat yellow.

4

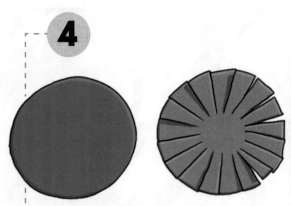

Cut out lots of small circles from colored cardstock. These will be flowers. Cut the edges, as shown, to make petals.

5

Glue the flowers
around your hat.

6

Glue some balls of tissue paper into the centers
of the flowers. Tie a big bow of ribbon and
glue it to your hat. Now your hat is ready!

CUTE

Bunny Mask

Did you know rabbits live in groups? Hop to it and make some bunny masks with your friends!

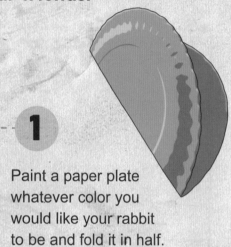

1

Paint a paper plate whatever color you would like your rabbit to be and fold it in half.

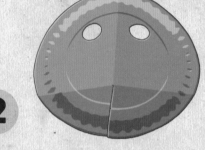

2

Unfold, then make a short slit along the crease. Use the end of a pencil to make holes for your scissors, then cut out two holes for eyes.

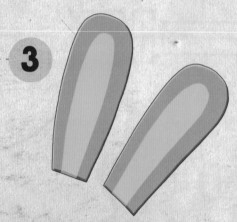

3

Cut out a pair of ears from cardstock and paint them to match your rabbit. You could paint the middle of the ears pink.

4

Paint the bottom of the mask a different color. Fold the bottom of the cut end inward so the pieces overlap. Glue into position. Glue on the ears and fold them forward.

Attach a piece of
elastic from one
side of the back
to the other.

**Handy
Hint**
You can add
some eyelashes
to the bottom of
the eyes, too.

6

Cut out a felt nose,
eyebrows, and some
whiskers. Glue them
into position. Put on
your mask and you
are ready to hop, hop,
hop away!

Sailboat

You will need

One paper plate
One paper bowl
Red and blue paint
Corrugated cardstock
Cardboard
One straw

1 To make the hull, glue a paper plate to the top of a paper bowl.

2 Paint the hull red. Cut out a circle of corrugated cardstock and glue to the top for the deck.

3 Cut out two triangles from cardboard—one must be slighter bigger than the other. Paint blue to make sails.

4 Glue your sails to a straw, as shown.

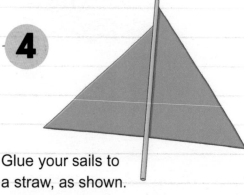

5 Make a hole with a pencil in the deck and glue the straw mast in place. Add some more detail to the sails, like stripes and a flag. Now it's time to set sail on the seven seas!

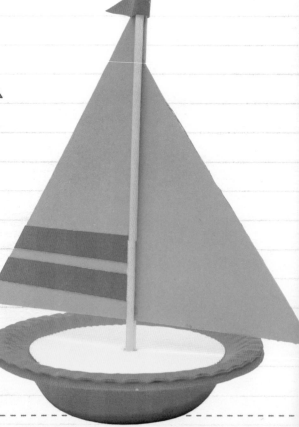

Bug Hat

Is it a bug? Is it a hat? It's both —and it will look great on you!

You will need

One paper bowl
Red and black paint
Two googly eyes
Black and yellow felt
Elastic

1

Paint the outside of a paper bowl red.

2

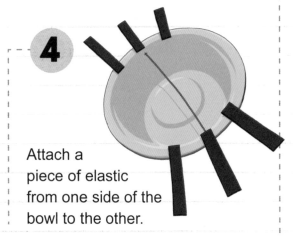

Paint on a black head and some spots.

3

To make legs, cut six strips of black felt and glue them to the body, as shown.

4

Attach a piece of elastic from one side of the bowl to the other.

5

Cut out some circles of felt (slightly bigger than the googly eyes) and glue the eyes to them. Glue to the bug. Why not repeat the steps to make different types of bugs?

Hot-Air Balloon

You will need

Two paper plates
One paper bowl
Paint, including brown
String
Tape
Ribbon

1

Paint a bright design
onto two plates so they match.

2

Paint a paper bowl
brown. Use the end
of a pencil to make four
evenly spaced holes around
the rim. Tie a piece of string
in each of the holes.

3

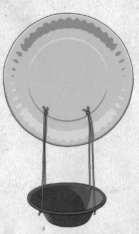

Tape the free
ends of the
strings to the
inside of one
of the plates.

4

Glue the other
plate to the first
plate, trapping
the string
between them.

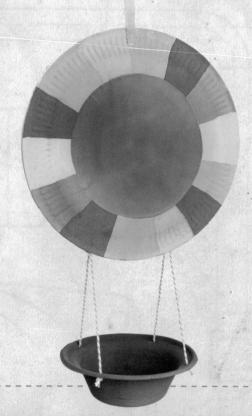

5

Glue a loop of ribbon to the top of
the balloon so you can hang it up.
Now decide which of your lucky
toys is going in the basket!

UFO

Is there anybody out there?
Make a spaceship and find out!

1

Glue two large
paper plates together
and paint them dark blue.

2

Paint a small bowl light
blue and glue it to the
top of the plates.

3

Cut some windows
from cardstock and draw on lots
of aliens. Glue the windows to
the small bowl on the UFO.

4

Add some shiny
paper circles to
the top plate. Tape
some thread to the
top of your UFO
to hang it in the
air. Your UFO is
ready to beam back
to Mars—but be
careful that it doesn't
take you with it!

Angel

This angel is pretty as can be—why not make two or even three!

You will need

One paper plate
One foam ball
Paint
One mini cake case
Two gold foil doilies
One cardboard tube
Shiny paper

1 Cut a paper plate in half. Make one half into a cone by folding the two points of the semi-circle into the center. Glue into position and paint it a bright color.

2 Paint the foam ball any skin tone. Use the end of a pencil to make a hole in it. Glue the point of the cone into the hole.

3 Add the mini cake case to the head for hair. Draw some features on the face and decorate the cone body with the gold doily.

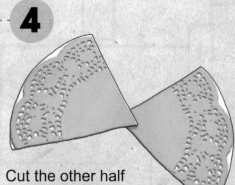

4 Cut the other half plate in two. These will be the wings. Add some pieces of gold doily to decorate them.

5

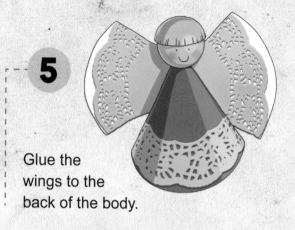

Glue the wings to the back of the body.

6

Cut a small ring from a cardboard tube and cover with shiny paper, for a halo.

7

Glue the halo in place to complete your angel. She would look lovely on top of a Christmas tree!

Handy Hint

Use glitter paint to add extra details to your pretty angels.

Monkey

Love monkeying around?
If you do, you'll have lots of
fun making this mischievous
friend. Just like you, monkeys
love to play!

You will need

One large paper bowl

One small paper bowl

One paper plate

Brown, beige, and
pink paint

Cardboard

Two googly eyes

One bottle top

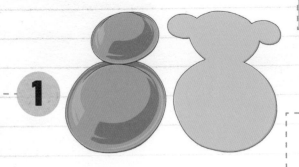

1 Draw around the paper bowls
onto a piece of cardboard. Add
two circles at the top for ears.
Cut out the shape. Glue the
two bowls to the cardboard.

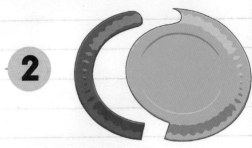

2 Cut the grooved edge
from a paper plate
for the monkey's
tail. Paint brown.

3 Paint the
monkey's body.
Give it brown
fur and a beige
face and tummy.
Paint the middle
of the ears pink.

4 Use the cardboard to cut
out a pair of legs and arms.
Paint to match the body.

48

5

Glue the tail, arms, and legs to the back of the body.

Handy Hint

Never throw away leftover cardstock. Keep it for projects, or if it cannot be used, recycle it.

6

Paint on a smile and glue on a pair of googly eyes and a bottle top nose. Your monkey is ready to play!

Dragon

1

Glue a strip of cardboard to the top edges of a small and large bowl.

2

Glue another small and another large bowl onto the top.

3

Cut out a crescent shape from the edge of a large plate. This will be the tail.

4

Glue the tail to the body. Paint it all red.

5

Paint a small paper plate red. Cut it in half, then cut out three semicircles along the straight edge of each piece to make wings.

6

Glue the wings in place.

7

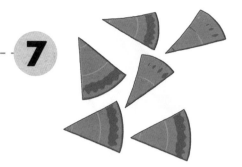

Cut six segments from a small plate and paint red.

8

Glue four segments to the base for feet. Glue two onto the head for crests. Add some details to the wings and body.

9

Glue two bottle tops to the head. Glue the eyes onto the bottle tops. Cut out some teeth from white cardstock and glue them in place. Watch out—your scary dragon is ready to breathe fire!

Handy Hint

If you do not have bottle tops, use pieces of painted cardstock or red felt.

Dotted Frog

What is spotted, dotted, and goes hoppity, hoppity? A little green frog, of course!

You will need

Three paper bowls
One cardboard tube
Green and yellow paint
White cardstock
Two googly eyes
One small paper plate

1

Glue two paper bowls together and paint them green.

2

Cut off a section from a cardboard tube and glue to the bowls, as shown. Paint the cardboard tube green.

3

Paint another bowl green. Place it on top of the cardboard tube and glue it into position.

4

Cut two circles from the cardstock. They should be slightly larger than the googly eyes. Paint them green. Glue the eyes to the circles.

5

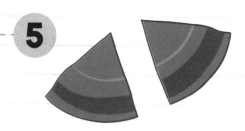

Cut two triangles from a small paper plate, for the frog's feet. Paint the triangles green.

6

Glue the eyes and feet in place. Paint the frog's belly pale green.

7

Add some dots to decorate your frog. Then make your frog hoppity-hop away!

RIBBET

RIBBET

Handy Hint

Let your paint dry completely before gluing the pieces together.

Wiggly Snake

Wiggle, wiggle, wiggle.
This colorful snake
will make you giggle!

You will need

Two paper plates
Paint
Cardboard
Red and blue cardstock
Two googly eyes

1

Cut a paper plate in half and cut away the middle sections so you are left with the grooved edges. Repeat this with another plate.

2

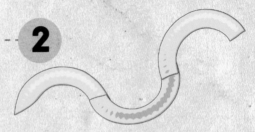

Glue the pieces together, as shown. You can add extra pieces if you want a really long snake. Make the tail pointed.

3

Paint the snake bright colors.

4

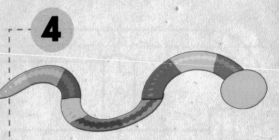

Cut out a large circle of cardboard and paint. Glue to the non-pointed end for the head. Add scaly details.

5

Cut a forked strip of red cardstock for the tongue. Cut out some circles of blue cardstock (slightly bigger than the googly eyes) and glue the eyes to them. Glue these to the head.

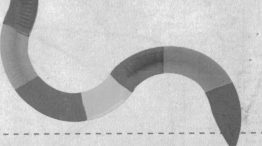

Christmas Tree Garland

Bring some festive cheer into your home with this colorful garland.

You will need

One paper plate
Paint, including green
Brown cardstock
Ribbon

1

Cut a paper plate into six sections.

2

Paint the sections green. Paint on lots of baubles.

3

Cut strips of brown cardstock for the trunks and glue them to the backs of the trees.

4

Glue a long piece of ribbon to the backs of the trees to join them together.

5

Hang your garland in a window to make a festive decoration.

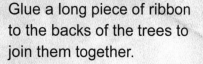

Peacock

You'll be proud as a peacock when you have made this pretty bird!

You will need

Three paper plates

Paint, including turquoise and yellow

Yellow and purple cardstock

Two googly eyes

1 Fold a paper plate as shown. Glue to hold in place. The folds will be at the back of the peacock.

2 Cut the bottom off another plate. Paint both plates turquoise.

3 Cut a third plate into sections, as shown. Paint them a darker shade of turquoise.

4 Fan out the plate sections. Glue them to the plate with the flat base. This is the peacock's tail.

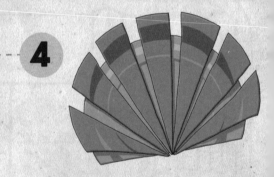

5 Glue the folded plate to the tail.

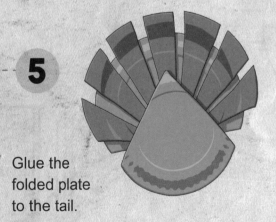

6

Cut out a semi-circle for the peacock's feet from the yellow cardstock. Cut out a diamond for the beak.

7

Glue the yellow feet to the back of the body. Then glue the beak in place. Cut out some circles of purple cardstock (slightly bigger than the googly eyes). Glue the eyes to the cardstock and then glue in place.

8

Cut out some circles from yellow cardstock and paint on some different colored details.

9

Glue the circles to your peacock's tail feathers to finish it off.

Handy Hint

Use clothespins to hold pieces in place while waiting for them to dry.

Fairy Toadstool

Make this fun toadstool for little fairies!

You will need

One paper bowl
Red, white, yellow, and blue paint
One paper cup

1 Paint a paper bowl red. When dry, add some white spots.

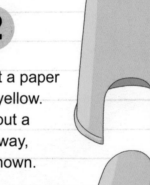

2 Paint a paper cup yellow. Cut out a doorway, as shown.

3 Glue the bowl to the cup.

4 Paint on some windows. Leave your toadstool on a window ledge so fairies can visit!

Jellyfish

This pink sea creature will look great hanging in your room.

1

Paint the paper bowl a pale color.

2

When dry, paint on different colored spots. Make some of them overlap.

3

Glue on a pair of googly eyes.

4

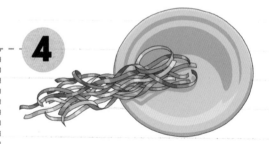

Cut different lengths of curly gift ribbon. Tie them together at one end and tape them to the underside of the jellyfish.

5

Tape a length of elastic to the top of the bowl. Gently tug on it to watch your jellyfish bounce up and down.

Seahorse

Shy and sweet, seahorses are one of the wonders of the seven seas. Why not decorate your house with this underwater beauty?

You will need

Three paper plates
Paint
Cardboard
Felt
One googly eye

1

Cut out a head shape from a paper plate, as shown.

2

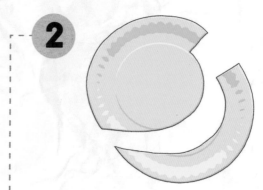

Cut a tail from another plate.

3

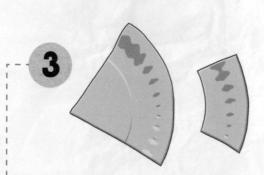

Cut some fins from the pieces of plate left over in step 2. Paint all the pieces and another plate the same color.

4

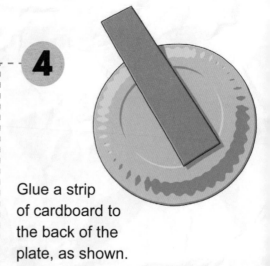

Glue a strip of cardboard to the back of the plate, as shown.

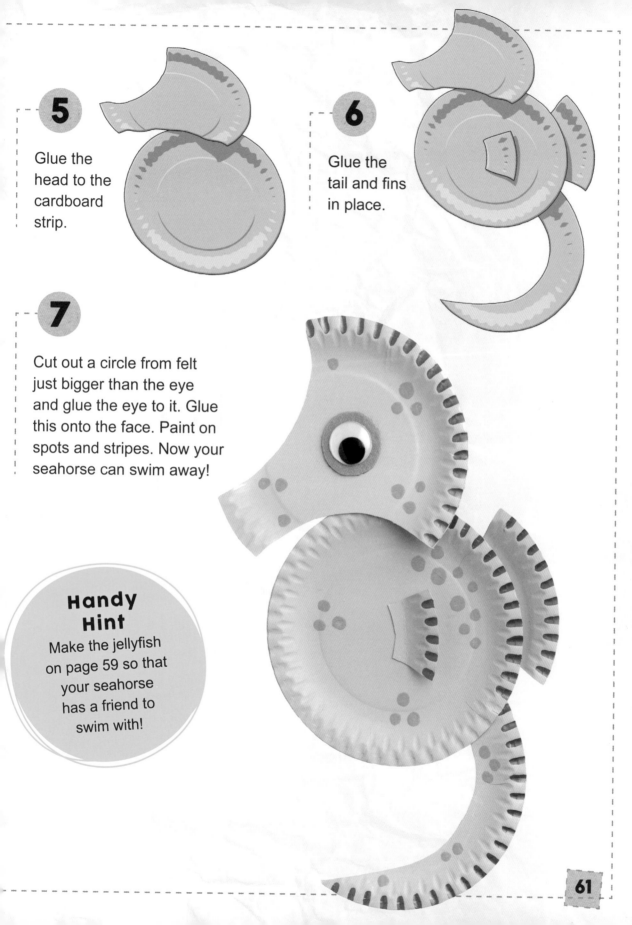

5

Glue the head to the cardboard strip.

6

Glue the tail and fins in place.

7

Cut out a circle from felt just bigger than the eye and glue the eye to it. Glue this onto the face. Paint on spots and stripes. Now your seahorse can swim away!

Handy Hint

Make the jellyfish on page 59 so that your seahorse has a friend to swim with!

Wise Owl

This bright and colorful owl makes a perfect nighttime friend. Hoot, hoot!

You will need

One large paper plate

Cardboard

Two small paper plates

Two paper bowls

Purple, lilac, turquoise, and yellow paint

Purple and yellow cardstock

Two googly eyes

1

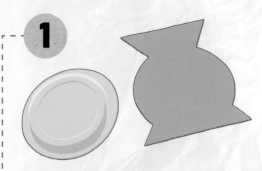

Draw around the large paper plate onto a thick piece of cardstock. Add shape to the top and bottom, as shown. Then cut out.

2

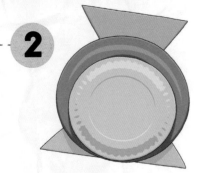

Paint the large plate purple and glue it onto the cardstock. Paint one small plate lilac and glue it onto the large plate. Paint the extra bit of cardstock at the bottom yellow to make the owl's feet.

3

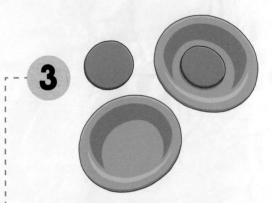

Paint the insides of two bowls turquoise. Cut out two circles of purple cardstock and glue one to the center of each bowl.

4

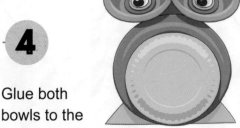

Glue both bowls to the top part of your cardstock shape. Cut out two circles from the yellow cardstock (slightly bigger than the googly eyes). Glue the eyes to the cardstock and then glue onto the purple circles.

5

Paint the second small plate purple, and then cut the plate in half.

6

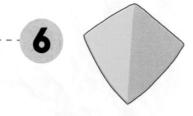

Cut a diamond shape from yellow cardstock for the beak.

7

Glue the wings and beak in place. Add some details to finish. Why not stick your wise owl onto your bedroom door?

HOOT
HOOT

Panda

Pandas love to eat bamboo! Can you make some to feed your hungry bear?

You will need

Cardboard
One paper plate
Two paper bowls
Black and white paint
Green cardstock
Pink felt
Two googly eyes

1

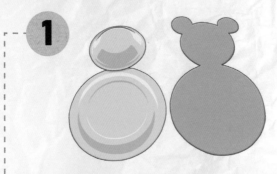

Draw around a paper plate and a paper bowl onto a piece of cardboard. Add ears, as shown. Now cut out the shape.

2

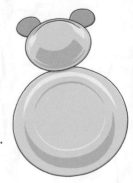

Glue the plate and bowl to the cardstock shape.

3

Glue another bowl upside-down to the plate, to make the panda's tummy.

4

Paint the top half of the body black. Give the panda black ears and a pair of big black blotches around the eyes.

5

Cut out pairs of legs and arms from cardboard. Paint them black.

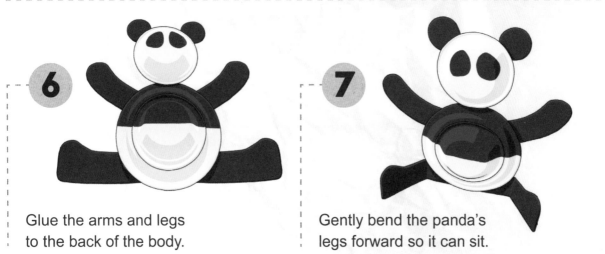

6

Glue the arms and legs to the back of the body.

7

Gently bend the panda's legs forward so it can sit.

8

Cut out some circles of green cardstock. Glue the eyes to these circles and then glue them onto the face. Cut out a nose from pink felt and glue it on. Draw on a mouth to finish your panda.

Handy Hint
Make your panda some bamboo from straws and cardstock.

Barking Dog Hand Puppet

Woof, woof, woof! Make this noisy puppet pal and entertain all your friends with its bark.

You will need

One small paper plate
One paper bowl
Pink and light and dark brown paint
Googly eyes
Bottle top
Cardstock
Red felt

1

Fold the plate in half, paint it pink on the inside and light brown on the outside. Paint the bowl light brown.

2

Glue half of the brown side of the plate to the top of the bowl.

3

Cut out some circles of cardstock (slightly bigger than the googly eyes) and paint the circles brown. Glue on the googly eyes. Fold back the bottom of the eye circle, to make a flat edge.

4

Add glue to the underside of the folded piece and glue the eyes to the head, as shown. Add a bottle top for the nose.

5

Cut out a pair of ears from cardstock and paint them dark brown.

6

Fold the bottom of the ears back and glue in place.

7

Cut out a tongue from red felt.

8

Glue the tongue inside the mouth and paint some spots on the head. Place your fingers into the bowl and your thumb under the mouth—now make your dog bark!

WOOF WOOF

Tree Shelf

Bring the outside indoors with this fun tree shelf. You can also keep pencils and pens inside it.

You will need

Twelve cardboard tubes

Paint

Paint the outsides of ten cardboard tubes green. Paint the insides contrasting colors.

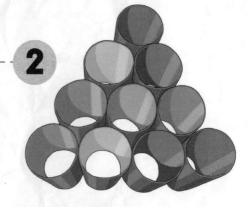

2

Glue the cardboard tubes together, to make a triangle.

Paint two more cardboard tubes brown and glue the sides together. Glue them to the base of your triangle.

You can make this tree as large as you like. Why not create an advent calendar and put little gifts in each cardboard tube?

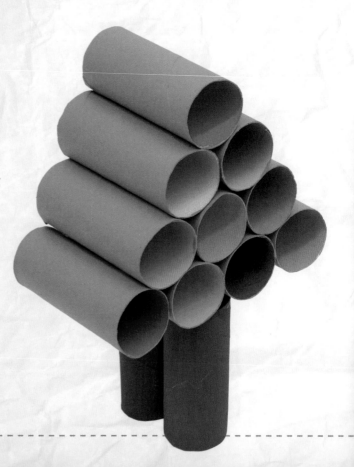

Totem Pole

You will need

Three cardboard tubes

Paint

Cardboard

Ten googly eyes

Felt

1

Paint three cardboard tubes different colors.

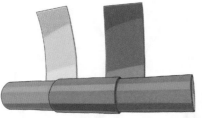

2

Cut and paint two strips of cardboard. Glue the cardboard around the tubes, making one long, sturdy tube.

3

Cut out a rectangle from cardboard. Cut a curved edge into one side of the rectangle, as shown. Paint. Cut two slits in the top of the first tube. Push the rectangle into the slits.

4

Cut a circle from the cardboard and paint it. Glue it over the top tube. Add felt circles, googly eyes, beaks, and scary mouths made from cardboard.

Toothy Shark

Is it safe to go swimming today? Well, this smiling, speeding shark won't harm you! You could put it in your bathroom to scare your guests, though!

You will need

One long cardboard tube
Gray and white paint
Blue and white felt
Two googly eyes

1

Slightly flatten a long cardboard tube so it is easier to cut. Cut out a V from one end. Keep this piece for the tail and fin.

2

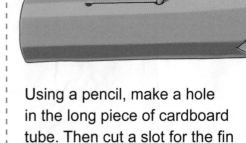

Using a pencil, make a hole in the long piece of cardboard tube. Then cut a slot for the fin to slide into.

3

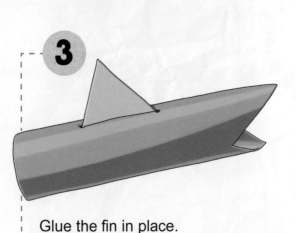

Glue the fin in place.

4

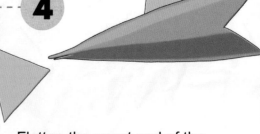

Flatten the uncut end of the cardboard tube and glue the edges together. Cut a slit in the tail and slide onto the back of the shark.

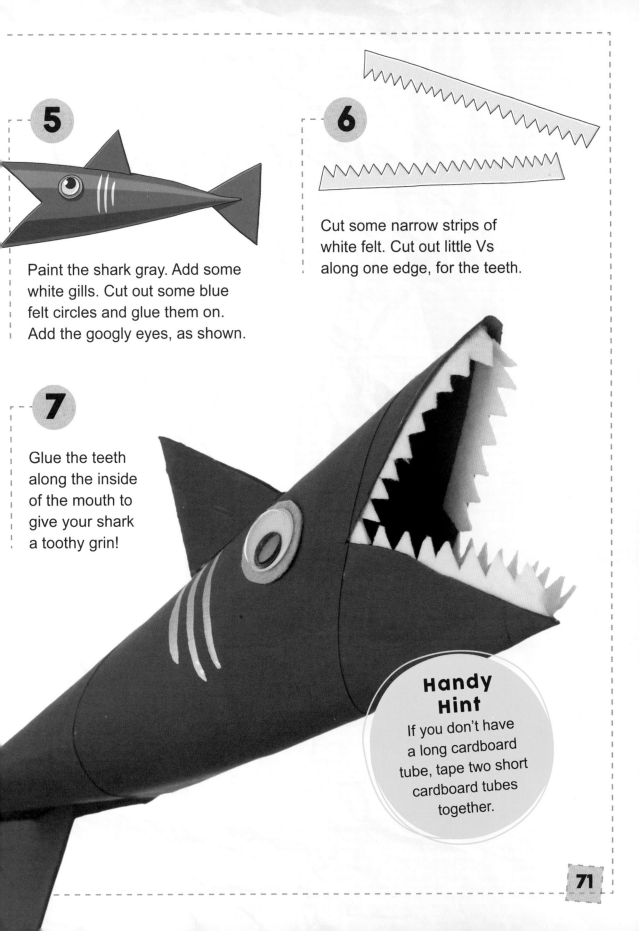

5

Paint the shark gray. Add some white gills. Cut out some blue felt circles and glue them on. Add the googly eyes, as shown.

6

Cut some narrow strips of white felt. Cut out little Vs along one edge, for the teeth.

7

Glue the teeth along the inside of the mouth to give your shark a toothy grin!

Handy Hint
If you don't have a long cardboard tube, tape two short cardboard tubes together.

Cute Duck

Quack, quack, quack!
This gorgeous little duck
is lots of fun to make and
even more fun to play with!

You will need

Three cardboard tubes

Yellow and orange paint

Cardboard

Googly eyes

1

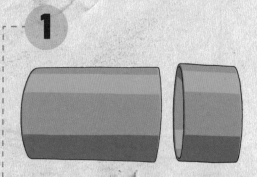

Cut a cardboard tube, as shown.
Keep the larger section for the duck's
legs and recycle the smaller piece.

2

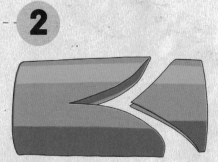

To make the head, cut out a
long, curved V from one end
of another cardboard tube.

3

Cut a large oval from another
cardboard tube. Glue the legs to
the underside. Hold in place with
clothespins until dry.

4

Glue the head to the
top of the body.

5

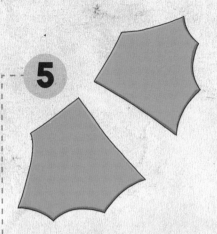

Cut out a pair of webbed
feet from the cardboard
and paint them orange.

6

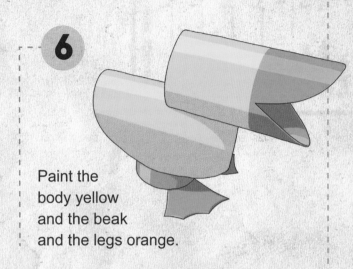

Paint the
body yellow
and the beak
and the legs orange.

QUACK
QUACK

7

Add some googly eyes
to finish off this cute
and colorful duck!

Tractor

1
Cut out a curved section from one end of a cardboard tube.

You will need

Two cardboard tubes
Paint
Cardboard
Blue cardstock
One tube cap

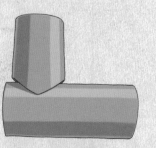

2
Glue the curved edge to the side of another cardboard tube.

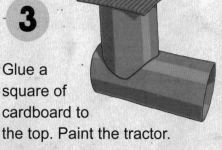

3
Glue a square of cardboard to the top. Paint the tractor.

4
For wheels, cut out two large and two small circles from cardboard, and paint them.

5
Glue the wheels to the sides of the tractor.

6
Add some cardstock rectangles for windows. Glue a tube cap to the front for the chimney.

Octopus

This amazing octopus looks so great that you'll feel you are exploring the deep for real!

You will need

One cardboard tube
Paint
Rubber band
Two googly eyes

1

Paint a cardboard tube inside and out. Use a contrasting color on the inside.

2

Put a rubber band around the cardboard tube, as shown. Cut eight evenly spaced slits up to the band.

3

Remove the band and roll each section around a pencil.

4

Now your octopus has eight legs.

5

Paint on some spots and a smile, and add some googly eyes to this eight-legged sea creature.

Racing Cars

1

To make the body of each car, use a pencil to make a hole for your scissors to cut a flap, as shown. Fold the flap backward. Paint the body.

2

Cut out four wheels from cardboard and paint black with a white middle.

3

Use a pencil to make a hole in the middle of each wheel. Place the wheels against the car and make holes with the pencil again.

4

Use metal fasteners to attach the wheels to the car.

5

Add a number and sporty stripes. Repeat the steps to make two more cars.

Pirate Pins

You will need

Five cardboard tubes

Paint, including pink and black

Felt

Paper

1

Divide your cardboard tubes into three sections. Paint the tops pink, the middles a bright color and the bottoms black. Add spots or stripes to the middles.

2

Cut out five large triangles of felt.

3

Wrap the long side of one triangle of felt around the pink end of one cardboard tube, and glue into position.

4

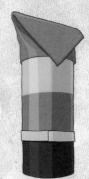

Fold down the tip of the triangle and glue. Repeat steps 3 and 4 on the other cardboard tubes.

5

Draw some features on each pirate. Scrunch up some paper to make balls, then see how many pins you can bowl over!

Stripy Zebra

Did you know that zebras have black and white stripes to help them to hide in a herd and keep them safe from predators?

1 Cut the corner off one end of two cardboard tubes.

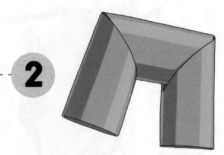

2 Glue the cardboard tubes to either end of another cardboard tube, as shown. They should slide into each other a bit.

3 Cut a ring from another cardboard tube and glue it to the body for the neck.

Handy Hint
The white paint must be completely dry before you add the stripes.

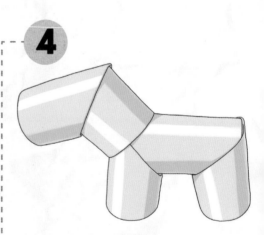

4 Cut the corner off another cardboard tube and glue it to the neck. This is the head. Paint your zebra white. When dry, paint on some stripes.

5

Cut a strip of black cardstock and glue it along the back of the neck for the mane. Cut a strip of black cardstock for the tail and glue it in place.

6

Cut out two ears from the cardstock as well as a circle to make the nose. Cut out some blue felt circles and add them to the googly eyes. Glue everything in place and paint on a smile.

STRIPY

Red Squirrel

You have probably seen lots of gray squirrels, but red squirrels are far rarer—and very, very beautiful, just like this one!

You will need

Two cardboard tubes

Orange, dark brown, black, and white paint

Two googly eyes

Cardstock

1

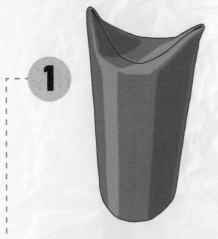

Push the sides of a cardboard tube into the center, to create a curved top. Paint light brown.

2

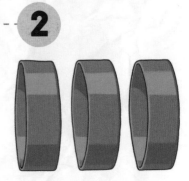

Cut three narrow rings from another cardboard tube. Paint light brown.

3

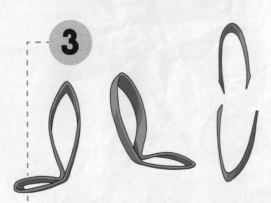

Bend two rings as shown, for the legs. Cut the last ring in half, for the arms.

4

Cut out a heart shape from cardstock and lightly fold down the middle. Glue on some googly eyes and paint on a small nose.

5

Paint on a white belly. Glue the face in place.

6

Glue the legs to either side of the body.

7

Cut out a tail from the cardstock, as shown. Paint it dark brown.

8

Cut a slit in the back of the cardboard tube and insert the tail. Glue to hold in position. Glue the arms to the body so that your squirrel is ready to look for some tasty nuts!

Daisies

Do you love flowers? If you do, you will adore these beautiful daisies. Make a bunch of them and put them in a vase.

You will need

Two cardboard tubes
Paint, including green
Rubber band
Cardboard
Tissue paper

1

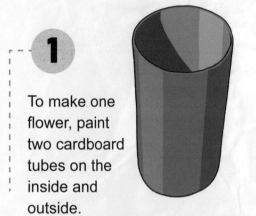

To make one flower, paint two cardboard tubes on the inside and outside.

2

Put a rubber band around the top of each tube, as shown. Cut slits up to the band.

3

Bend the pieces outward, to make petals. Cut one of the tubes, to make the diameter slightly smaller, and re-glue.

4

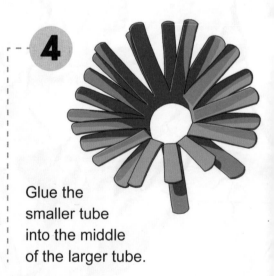

Glue the smaller tube into the middle of the larger tube.

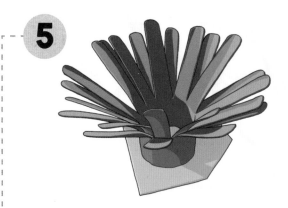

5

Glue the back of the daisy to a piece of cardboard. When dry, cut away the excess cardboard and paint it green.

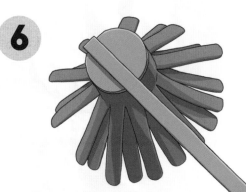

6

Glue a narrow strip of cardboard to the back of the daisy for the stem. Paint it green.

7

Scrunch up some tissue paper and glue it into the middle of the flower to finish off the pretty bloom.

Plane

Zoom, zoom! Up, up and away!
Take to the skies with this
spectacular flying machine.

You will need

One cardboard tube
Orange and blue paint
Cardboard
Blue cardstock
One metal fastener
Two bendy straws

1

For the
body, paint
a cardboard
tube orange.

2

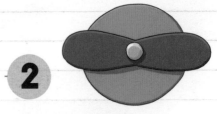

Cut a circle from cardboard
to fit the top of the cardboard tube.
Paint the circle orange. Then cut
a propeller from blue cardstock.
Use a metal fastener to attach the
propeller to the circle, as shown.

3

Glue the
circle to one
end of the cardboard tube.

4

Cut out two
rectangles from cardboard,
for the wings. Cut out three
smaller rectangles, each with one
curved corner, from cardboard.
Paint all the pieces blue.

5

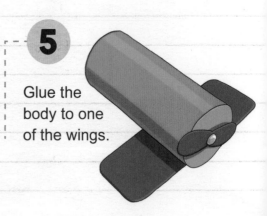

Glue the
body to one
of the wings.

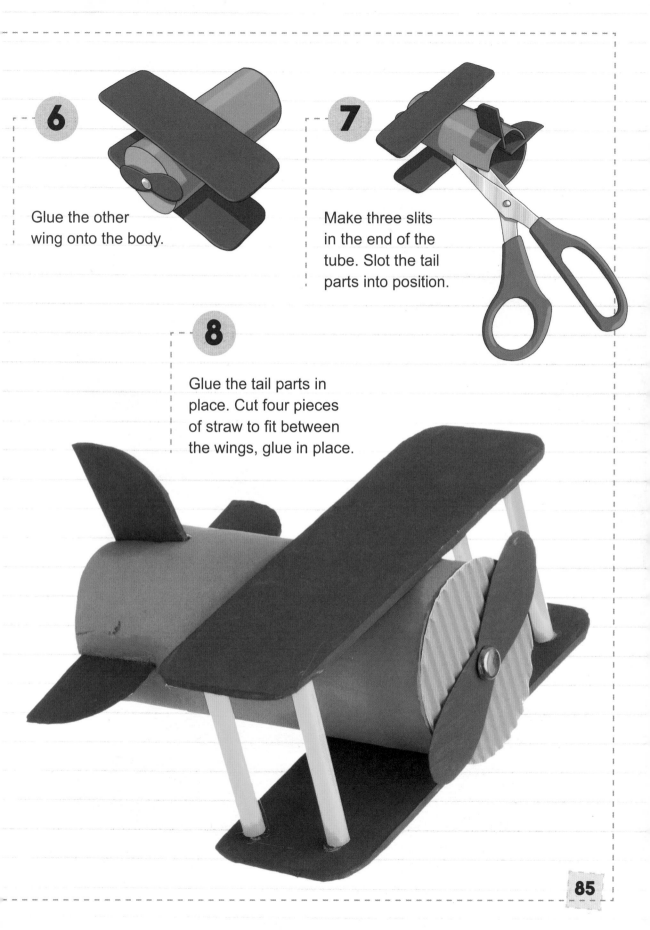

6 Glue the other wing onto the body.

7 Make three slits in the end of the tube. Slot the tail parts into position.

8 Glue the tail parts in place. Cut four pieces of straw to fit between the wings, glue in place.

Caterpillar

This cute and colorful caterpillar will brighten up any bedroom. Why not hang it from your ceiling?

You will need

Five cardboard tubes
Paint, including red
Ribbon
One foam ball
Two googly eyes
Two bendy straws

1 Paint some cardboard tubes different colors. When dry, cut the tubes into three sections.

2 Place the cut tubes side by side—mix up the colors. Glue a long piece of ribbon to the top of each tube.

3 Paint a tube red, and when dry, cut it into thin rings, as shown.

4

Glue the narrow red rings onto the ribbon. Turn over so the ribbon is on the bottom.

5

Paint a foam ball and glue it to the front of your caterpillar. Add some googly eyes.

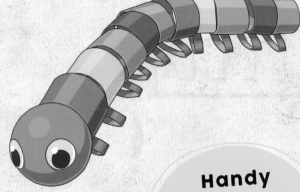

6

Use a pencil to make two holes on the top of the ball. Insert two short straws and glue in place. Your creepy, crawly caterpillar is ready!

Handy Hint

Allow the glue to dry completely before moving your caterpillar.

Mini Mice

Are you scared of mice? Well, there is nothing scary about these cuddly friends. You'll want to make lots and lots of them!

1 Flatten one end of a cardboard tube and glue the sides together.

2 Flatten the other end the opposite way to step 1, and glue the sides together. Repeat steps 1 and 2 with another cardboard tube.

3 Paint the mice, as shown—don't forget the noses! Cut out some ears and a tail from pink felt and glue in place.

4 Glue on some googly eyes and wait for the happy squeaks to begin!

Chinese Lanterns

You will need

One cardboard tube
Paint
Cardstock

1

Paint the inside and outside of a cardboard tube and cut it along its length.

2

Flatten the tube and fold in half lengthways. Cut slits from the folded edge, as shown. Don't cut to the top!

3

Re-roll the tube and glue the edges together.

4

Lightly compress the tube, to make the slits fold out.

5

Cut a thin strip of cardstock for a handle and glue to the top of the lantern. Use clothespins to hold in place.

6

Your lantern is ready. Make lots more lanterns and hang them up with string.

Dinosaur Desk Bins

You will need

Three long cardboard tubes

Five short cardboard tubes

Paint

Cardboard

Pink felt

Two googly eyes

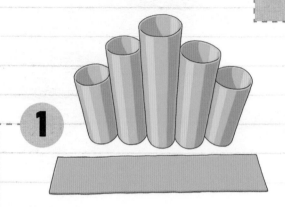

1 Cut the long cardboard tubes and two short tubes so that you have one long one, two shorter ones, and two even shorter ones. Paint them and line them up, as shown. Glue them to cardboard that is slightly longer than the row of tubes.

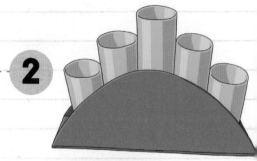

2 Cut out two semi-circles of cardboard. Paint them a contrasting color. Glue them to either side of the row of tubes.

3 Flatten the top of another tube, glue the sides together, and paint it the same color as the cardboard in step 2. This will be the tail.

4 Cut the top corner off a tube. Paint this and another tube in the same color as the cardboard in step 2.

5

Glue the tubes together, for the head.

6

Glue the head and tail in place.

7

Paint on some spots and a smile. Add some felt circles and the eyes. Your happy dinosaur is ready to help you tidy your desk!

DINO BINS

Train

Make this multi-colored train—it will be the best on any track.

You will need

Five cardboard tubes

Cardboard

Tube cap

Paint

Ribbon

1

Cut out a curved section from one end of a cardboard tube.

2

Glue the curved edge to the side of another tube.

3

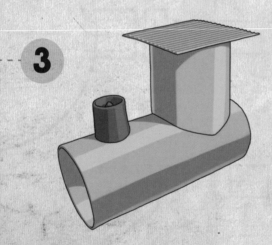

Glue a square of cardboard to the top. Paint the train engine a pretty bright color. Add a tube cap for the funnel, as shown.

Handy Hint

To make a circle, draw around a jar lid and cut out.

4

5

Paint three other tubes for the train cars. To make wheels, cut out four circles of cardboard for each car and six circles for the engine. Paint and glue them into position.

6

Make a long line of cars for the train to pull!

Cut some pieces of ribbon. Glue to the inside of the engine and cars, as shown.

CHOO
CHOO

Cool Castle

1 Paint all of the tubes. Cut and assemble the long cardboard tubes and seven of the short tubes to make a castle, as shown.

2 Cut two slits in one end of the last two cardboard tubes. These will be the turrets.

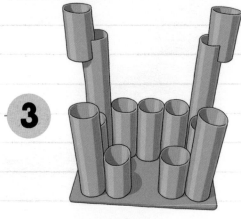

3 Slide the turrets over the towers. Glue all the tubes to a piece of thick green cardstock.

4 To make some roofs, cut a semi-circle of cardstock for each tower, shape it into a cone, and glue it in place. Paint the roofs.

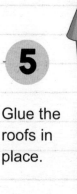

5 Glue the roofs in place.

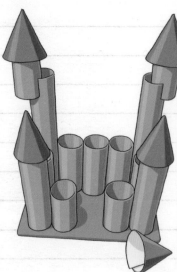

94

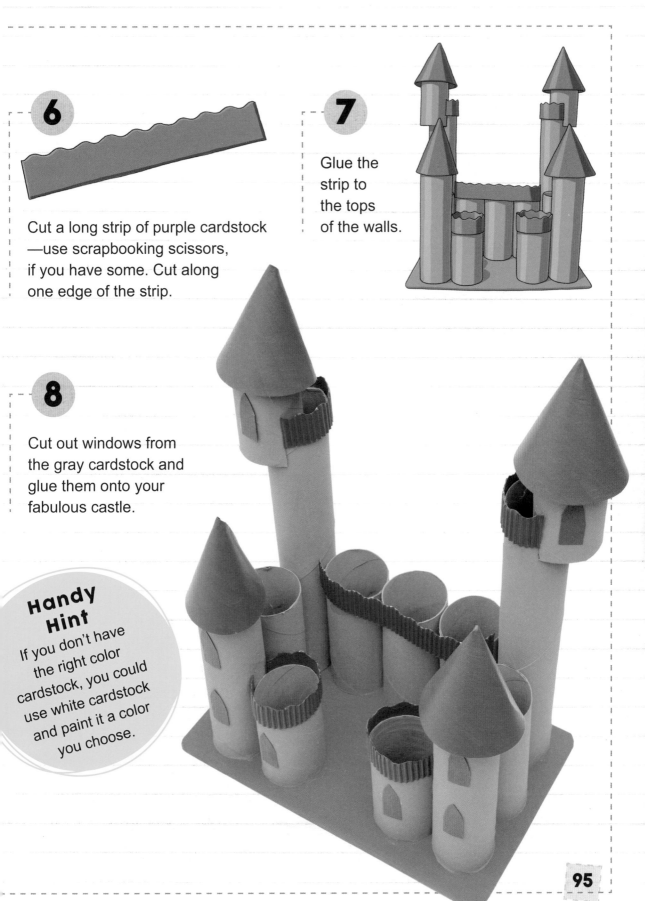

6

Cut a long strip of purple cardstock
—use scrapbooking scissors,
if you have some. Cut along
one edge of the strip.

7

Glue the
strip to
the tops
of the walls.

8

Cut out windows from
the gray cardstock and
glue them onto your
fabulous castle.

**Handy
Hint**
If you don't have
the right color
cardstock, you could
use white cardstock
and paint it a color
you choose.

95

Chickens

Cluck, cluck, cluck! These pretty, spotted chickens will brighten up any room. You could make a set and line them up on a shelf.

You will need

Two cardboard tubes
Paint
Red felt or cardstock
Yellow cardstock
Four googly eyes

1

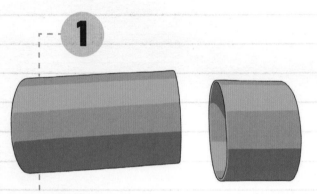

For each chicken, cut a cardboard tube, as shown. Use the longer pieces for your chickens and recycle the rest.

2

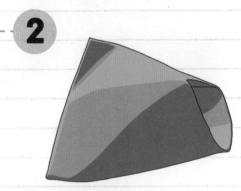

Flatten one end of each tube and glue it together.

3

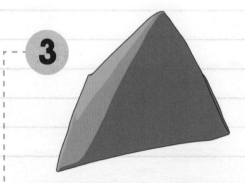

Flatten the other end of each tube the opposite way to step 2, and glue it together. Paint your chickens.

4

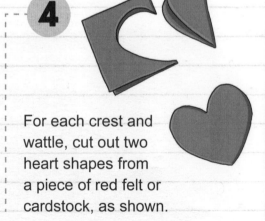

For each crest and wattle, cut out two heart shapes from a piece of red felt or cardstock, as shown.

5

Fold in half a piece of yellow cardstock and cut out a triangle, for the beak.

6

Glue the crest, wattle, and beak in place.

crest

wattle

7

Paint your chicken. Add spots and googly eyes and cluck, cluck, cluck!

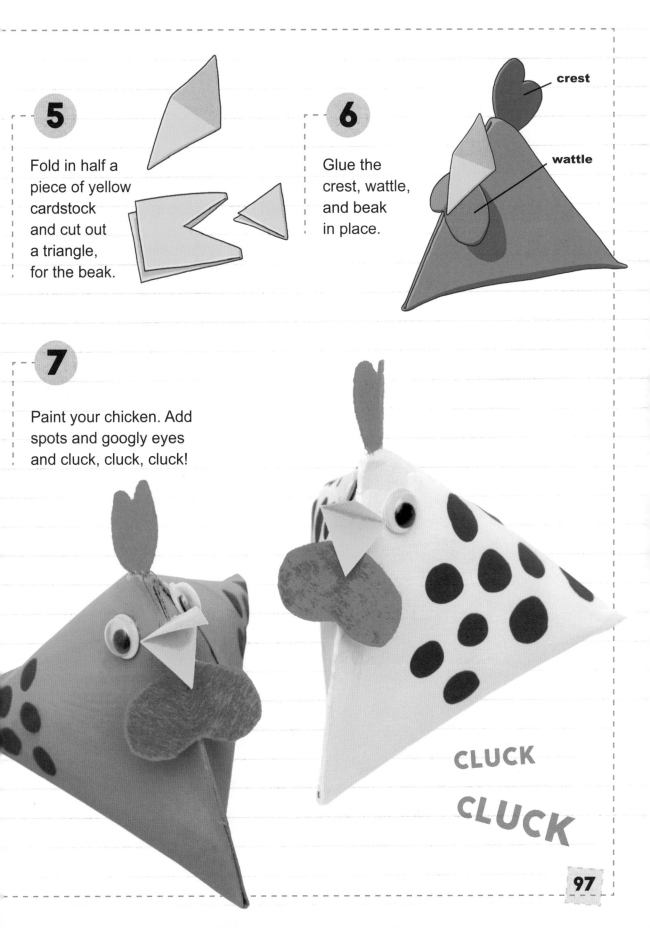

CLUCK

CLUCK

Friendly Fox

1

Fold the top of a cardboard tube, as shown. Glue in place.

2

Paint the top part of the tube brown and the underneath white. Paint on a black nose.

3

Cut out two triangles from the cardstock, for ears. Paint them brown and glue them in place.

4

Add two googly eyes, whiskers, and other details. Quick, hide the chickens!

Coral Reef and Fish

1

Glue an acorn cup to each pine cone. Paint the cone and acorn cup or leave natural.

2

Glue a shell to each side and the end of each cone. Push them between the cone scales.

3

For each fish, paint two acorn cups white. Add a black dot to each one. Glue them onto the cone. Tie string around the cone and then tie into a loop.

4

Paint a branch orange to make it look like coral. Draw on markings in felt-tip pen. Hang your fish on the piece of coral.

Owls

Pine cones can be male or female. Female pine cones contain seeds. The seeds fall to the ground with the cone and may grow into a new tree.

You will need

Small and large pine cones

Felt of different colors, including yellow

Acorn cups

Dried beans

Branch

Adhesive putty (such as Blu Tack™)

1

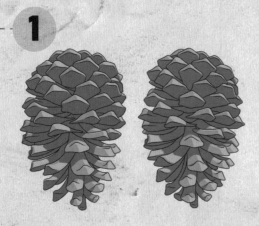

Paint some of the pine cones and leave others unpainted.

2

For each cone, cut a diamond from felt. Make it about the same length as the cone.

3

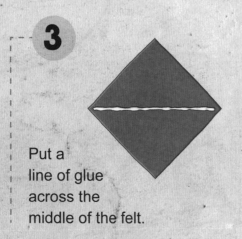

Put a line of glue across the middle of the felt.

4

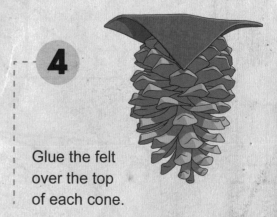

Glue the felt over the top of each cone.

5

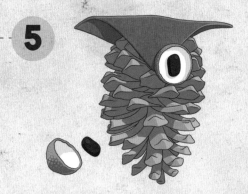

For each cone, paint the insides of two acorn cups white. Glue a dried bean into each one. Stick them to the front of the cone.

6

For each owl, cut out a beak from yellow felt and glue in place.

7

Sit the owls on a branch. If they fall off, attach them with adhesive putty.

HOOT
HOOT

Handy Hint
Large owls may need googly eyes instead of acorn and bean eyes.

Penguins

Helicopter seeds are the seed pods from maple and sycamore trees. They spin as they fall from the trees.

You will need

A large, rough flat stone
Two smooth pebbles
Pistachio nut shells
Dried peas
Two pairs of helicopter seeds
Adhesive putty

1

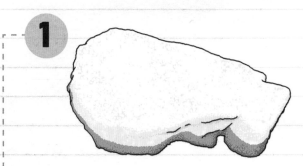

Paint the rough stone white. Add a pale blue edge. This is your iceberg.

2

Paint a white oval on the front of each pebble. When dry, paint the rest of both pebbles black.

3

Paint two half pistachio nut shells yellow. Glue them onto each pebble for beaks. Glue on two dried peas for eyes and add a black dot to each.

4

Paint the helicopter seeds black and glue one pair to the back of each pebble for wings.

5

Use a cool melt glue gun or adhesive putty to stick the pebble penguins to the iceberg.

Hedgehog

You will need

Brown felt
Pine cones
Acorn cups
Dried beans

1

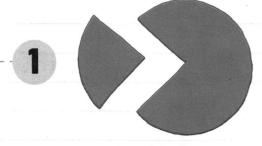

Cut out a circle from felt. Cut out a quarter section and keep it to make the ears later.

2

Twist the rest of the felt into a cone. Glue it in place.

3

Cut out a pair of ears from the leftover felt quarter.

4

Glue the ears to the inside of the felt cone.

5

Glue the felt cone to the top of the pine cone.

6

Paint an acorn cup black and glue to the tip of the felt cone for a nose. Glue on two dried beans for eyes. Paint a white dot onto each eye and your hedgehog is ready to scurry away.

Birds

Choose bright colors for your birds or try to re-create birds that you see outside your home.

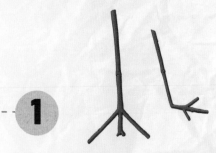

1 Cut two thin sticks with side shoots the same length. Carefully bend the sticks upward just above the side shoots to make them into feet.

2 Paint the foam ball. Use the tip of a pencil to make two holes, close together, in the ball. Push the feet into the holes.

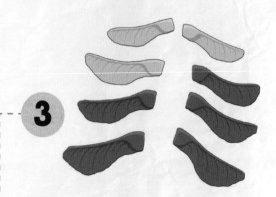

3 Cut four helicopter seed pairs in half. Paint them or leave a natural color.

4 Make a pair of wings by gluing together three of the half helicopter seeds as shown.

5 Glue the wings to each side of the ball.

6 Make a tail with the remaining two half helicopter seeds.

7

Cut a slit in the back of the ball. Put glue onto the narrow part of the tail and push into the slit.

8

Paint half a pistachio nut shell yellow. Push the edge of it into the front of the ball. Remove it and add a dab of glue before pushing it back into place.

9

Add a pair of dried bean eyes. Follow the steps again to make a flock of birds.

Handy Hint
If your birds will not stand up, press their feet into small pieces of adhesive putty.

Tortoise

You will need

Foam ball
Four cockle shells
Half coconut shell
Limpet shells
Two acorn cups

1

Paint a foam ball and four cockle shells green.

2

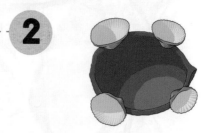

Turn the coconut shell over. Glue the cockle shells to the edge of the coconut shell to make the feet.

3

Turn the coconut shell back up the right way. Glue on the foam ball for the head.

4

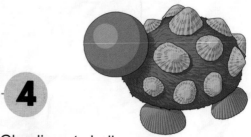

Glue limpet shells over the coconut shell.

5

For the eyes, paint two acorn cups green. Add a big black dot and a smaller white dot to each cup.

6

Glue the eyes to the head. Add yellow spots and a smile.

Star

1

Cut five sticks to the same length.

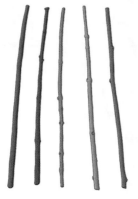

2

Make them into a "W" shape. Wrap a rubber band around the sticks that cross over each other.

3

Take the two outer sticks and pull them toward each other so that they cross over.

4

Put the fifth stick across the top to join the two stick ends. Wrap rubber bands around both ends of this stick. Tie yarn around the sticks that cross over each other in the middle of the star to strengthen it.

5

Wrap yarn around the star's points to decorate it.

Sheep

In the winter when sheep have their full, fleecy coats, look for tufts of fleece caught on fences or bushes.

You will need

Thick stick	String
Saw (adult use)	Foam egg
Thick cardstock	Sheep fleece
Long pine cone with wide open scales	Two mussel shells
	Three small shells

1 Ask an adult to help cut four short pieces of a thick stick. Glue these stick legs to a rectangle of thick cardstock.

2 Tie the pine cone to the cardstock with string. Wrap the string around the cone at least three times to make it secure.

3 Turn the model over so the legs are at the bottom. Paint the foam egg black. Glue it to the wide end of the cone.

4 Poke pieces of fleece into the gaps between the scales of the cone. Use a pencil to push it deep into the cone.

5

Continue covering the cone with fleece.

6

Make two small indents on the top of the head. Glue a mussel shell into each hole for ears.

7

Glue more fleece between the ears. Add two small shells for eyes and one for a nose. Add a black dot with a felt-tip pen onto each eye. Your sheep can now go off to graze.

Handy Hint

Put your fleece in a bowl filled with warm water and dishwashing soap. Let it soak for 30 minutes to remove any grease.

Dinosaur

1

Blow up a balloon and tie the end. Use tape to attach it to a jar. Dip strips of newspaper into your glue mix and lay them on the balloon. Cover the top half of your balloon with three layers of paper.

2

When dry, pop the balloon. Paint the papier mache purple. Trim the edge of the bowl shape and cut out a semicircle from the edge.

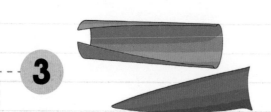

3

Cut out a long triangle from the cardboard tube. Paint it purple to make a tail.

4

Glue or tape the tail into the semicircle in the body.

5

Use the tip of a pencil to make holes along the middle of the body and tail. Glue short lengths of thin stick into the holes.

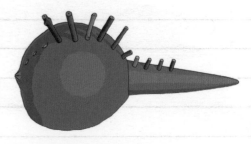

6

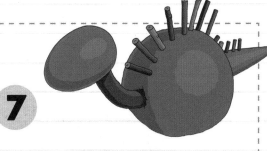

Make a hole with a pencil in the front end of the body. Then use scissors to cut slits out from the hole.

7

Paint the egg purple. Make a hole in the thick end of the egg and glue it to the bent stick. Glue the stick into the hole in the body.

8

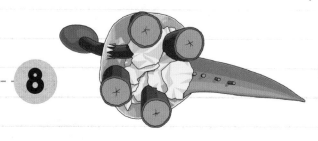

Ask an adult to help cut four short lengths of a thick stick. Glue these to the inside edge of the body. Stuff the body with scrunched up newspaper to make it stronger.

9

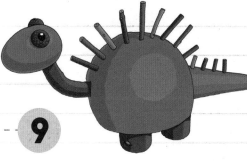

Paint black circles on two acorn cups. Add a white dot to each. Glue these eyes to the head.

ROARRR!
ROAR!

10

Paint on some yellow spots and your dinosaur is free to roam.

Lion Mask

Look for fallen leaves in fall. Press them flat inside a heavy book to dry. They will be ready to use after about a week.

1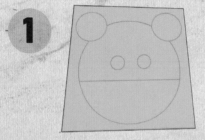

Draw around a plate (about 12 inches or 30 cm across) on yellow cardstock. Next, draw around a jar to make two ears. Add two circles in the middle for eyes. Draw a line below the eyes.

2

Cut out the mask. Use a pencil to make a hole for your scissors when you cut out the eyes. Paint the inside of the ears pink.

3

Draw a circle on white cardstock larger than the plate you used. Draw another circle inside it, making it smaller than the plate and off-center.

4

Cut out the circles and cut out a section from the bottom. Use the tip of a pencil to make a hole in both sides. Tie a piece of elastic through the holes.

5

Glue leaves all around the outside, so they overhang the edge.

6

Continue with more leaves, overlapping them until you only have a small area of white cardstock showing.

7

Put some glue on the white areas of cardstock, then glue the yellow piece on top.

8

Cut out two round shapes of white cardstock. Glue to the bottom left and right of the mask.

9

Cut two leaves in half and glue above the eyes for eyebrows.

10

Cut out a nose from black felt and glue it on. Draw on some whiskers. Put on your mask and you are ready to roar!

Puppets

Dry flowers for your puppets by pressing them between the pages of a heavy book.

You will need

Poppy seed heads	Cotton wool
Paper straws	Thin sticks with side shoots
Colored cardstock, printer size	Shells, dried seed pods, helicopter seeds, and flowers
Clothespins	Googly eyes

1

Paint the poppy seed head any skin colour. Glue the stem inside a paper straw.

2

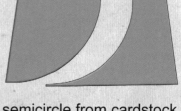

Cut out a semicircle from cardstock. Keep the offcuts for the arms.

3

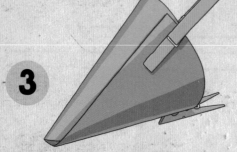

Glue the semicircle of cardstock into a cone shape, leaving a small hole at the top. Use clothespins to hold in place while the glue dries.

4

Slide the straw into the cone. Add a dab of glue to keep it in place.

5

Push cotton wool into the cone around the straw to keep it from moving.

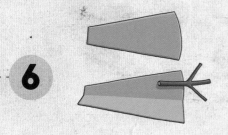

6

Cut out a pair of arms from the offcuts of cardstock. Glue on the sticks with side shoots to the top half of the arms. These are the hands. Fold the arms in half and glue to trap the hands inside.

7

Glue the arms to the back of the cone.

8

Add shells, helicopter seeds, and other seed pods to the head to make hair and features.

9

Add seed pods or dried flowers to the body.

10

Glue on googly eyes. Make more puppets using different seed pods and put on a show.

Bugs

You will need

Two whole walnuts
Two cockle shells
Four dried lentils
Bark

1

Paint one walnut shell half red, half black for a ladybug. Paint the other walnut shell half yellow, half black for a bee.

2

Paint black stripes on the yellow part of the bee. For the ladybug, paint the narrow end black and add black spots to the rest of the body.

3

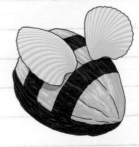

Glue on two small cockle shells to the bee for wings.

4

Stick dried lentils to each bug for eyes. Draw black dots on the lentil eyes and add a smile to the bee. Place the bugs on their woody home.

Handy Hint

If you cannot find bark for your bugs' home, a log would work well, too.

cacti

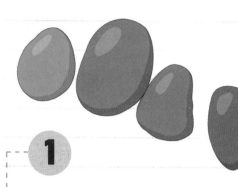

1

Paint your pebbles different shades of green.

2

Add some detail, such as spots or stars, to look like spikes.

3

Paint some beechnuts to look like flowers.

4

Put dry sand or gravel into a flower pot. If your pot has a hole in the bottom, cover it with tape first.

5

Push your pebble cacti into the gravel. Then glue on your flowers to create a beautiful display.

Lizard

Lizards are cold blooded. This means they need heat from the Sun to warm their bodies. Let your lizard bask on a warm windowsill.

1 Ask an adult to cut a section of the thick stick for the body. Paint the stick and the egg green. Glue the egg to the stick.

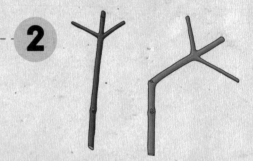

2 Cut two long, thin sticks with side shoots for the back legs. Carefully bend the sticks to the side about halfway along the stem.

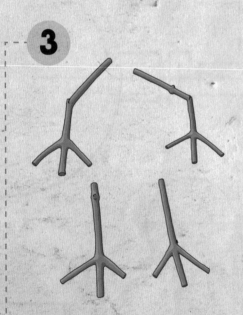

3 Cut another two sticks with side shoots. These need to be shorter than the back legs. Paint all the legs green.

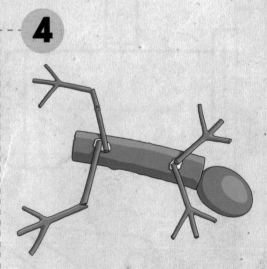

4 Use a cool melt glue gun to attach the legs to the body.

118

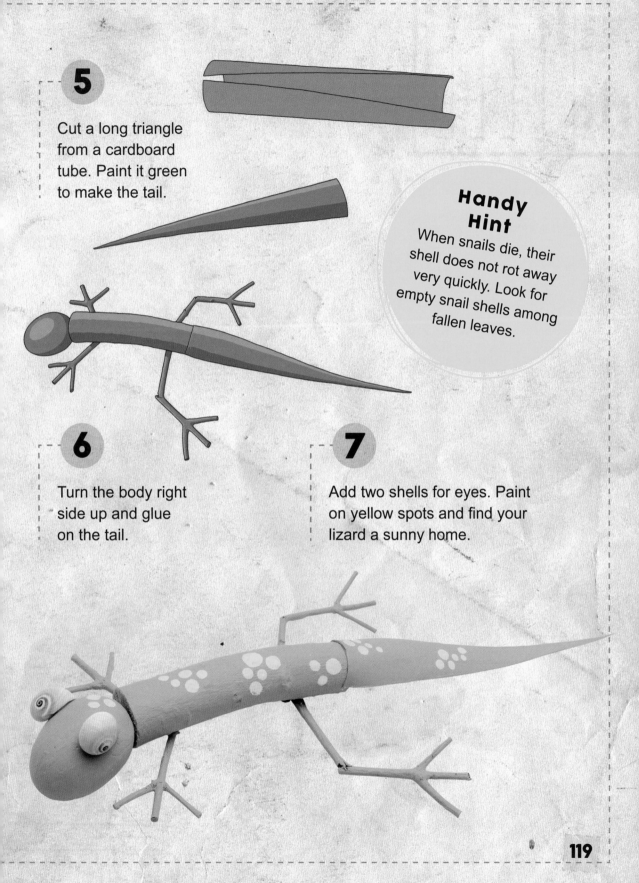

5

Cut a long triangle from a cardboard tube. Paint it green to make the tail.

Handy Hint
When snails die, their shell does not rot away very quickly. Look for empty snail shells among fallen leaves.

6

Turn the body right side up and glue on the tail.

7

Add two shells for eyes. Paint on yellow spots and find your lizard a sunny home.

Mushrooms

1

Paint some of the limpet shells red with white spots. Leave some shells their natural color.

2

Cut some thin, twisted sticks similar lengths to make the mushroom stems.

3

Push a piece of modeling clay into each shell. Push a stick stem into the clay.

4

On a thick stick, drill some holes that are slightly wider than the stick stems.

5

Add a dab of glue to each hole. Push in the mushroom stems. Your mushroom garden is complete.

Crab

You will need

Six cockle shells
Smooth pebble
Two snail shells
Two dried leaves
Cardstock
Two short, thin sticks

1

Paint six cockle shells bright orange.

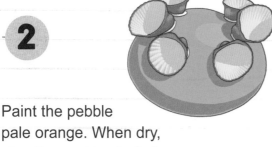

2

Paint the pebble pale orange. When dry, glue the cockle shells to the base for the feet.

3

Glue on two snail shells to the top of the pebble for eyes.

4

Glue two dried leaves to a piece of cardstock. Cut them out and then cut in half along the vein in the middle. Glue each one to a short, thin stick for claws.

5

Glue the claws to the top of the pebble. Paint on some yellow spots and add a smile. Look out for those pincers!

121

Reindeer

Reindeer live in cold places. They use their hooves to dig for food in the snow.

1

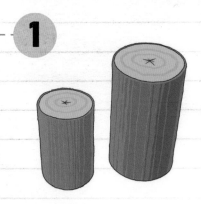

Ask an adult to cut the thickest log with a saw to make the body. From the narrow log, cut a section about three-quarters the length of the body. This will be the head.

2

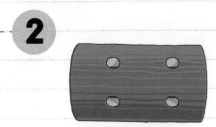

Get an adult to drill four holes in the body. They should be slightly bigger than your thin straight sticks and should be angled toward the middle of the body.

3

Turn the body over and drill another hole near one end. This should be angled toward the back of the body.

4

Cut four thin sticks the same length for the legs. Put a dab of glue into the four holes on the base of the body. Push the thin sticks into the holes.

5

Cut a thin stick shorter than the legs. Glue this into the top hole on the body to make a neck.

6

Take the head and drill a hole near one end. This should go straight down.

7

Turn the head over and drill two holes for the antlers. Make sure they are on the same end as the previous hole.

8

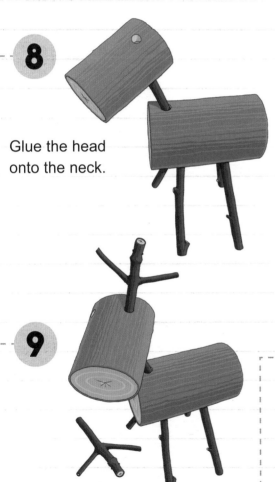

Glue the head onto the neck.

9

Glue the two sticks with side shoots into the holes. These are the antlers.

10

Stick on a pistachio shell for each ear. Paint an acorn cup black and glue on for the nose. Add two dried bean eyes and a cockle shell tail. Paint a white spot on each eye and add spots to the body and head.

Sun Picture Frame

1

Cut out two circles from thick cardstock. Make sure one circle is very slightly smaller than the other. Cut out a circle from the middle of the largest circle.

2

Paint the large circle yellow. This will be the frame.

3

Glue four long sticks around the frame.

4

Glue on more sticks. Space them evenly around the frame. Paint the ends of the sticks yellow.

5

Put some glue into every other gap between the sticks. Place different colored dried beans onto the glue.

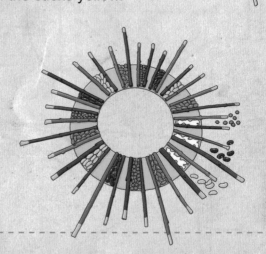

124

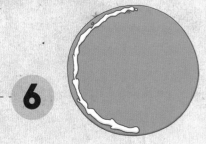

6 Put a line of glue halfway around the edge of the smaller circle.

7 Glue this circle to the back of your frame. Glue on a loop of ribbon so you can hang it up.

8 The unglued section at the back means you can slide your favorite picture into the frame.

Tree Frogs

Tree frogs can be green, gray, or brown, or very brightly colored. They live in hot parts of the world.

You will need

Long, thin sticks with side shoots

Short, thin sticks with side shoots

Smooth pebbles

Acorn cups

Yellow cardstock

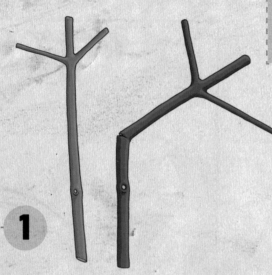

1

Cut two long, thin sticks with side shoots for the back legs. Carefully bend the sticks to the side about halfway along the stem. They may partially snap, which is fine.

2

Cut another two sticks with side shoots to make the front legs. These should be shorter than the back legs. Paint all the legs green, or leave natural.

3

Paint a pebble green or leave natural. Use a cool melt glue gun to attach the legs to the body.

4

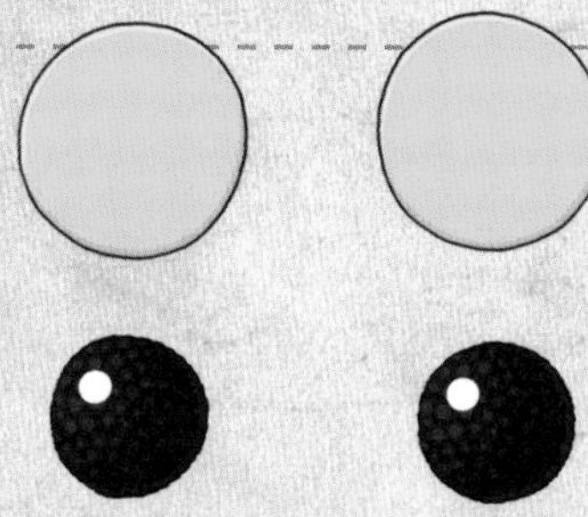

Paint two acorn cups black. Add a white dot to each. Cut out two circles from yellow cardstock. Make these slightly larger than the acorn cups.

5

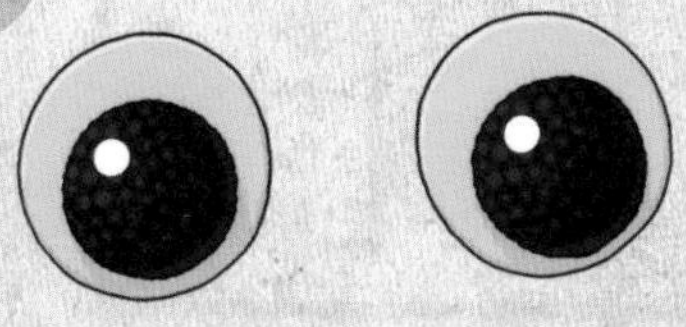

Glue the acorn cups to the circles to make the eyes.

6

Glue the eyes to the top of the body. Add some spots. Your frog is ready to hop off!

Handy Hint

Clean any soil from your pebbles by scrubbing them in dishwashing soap and warm water.

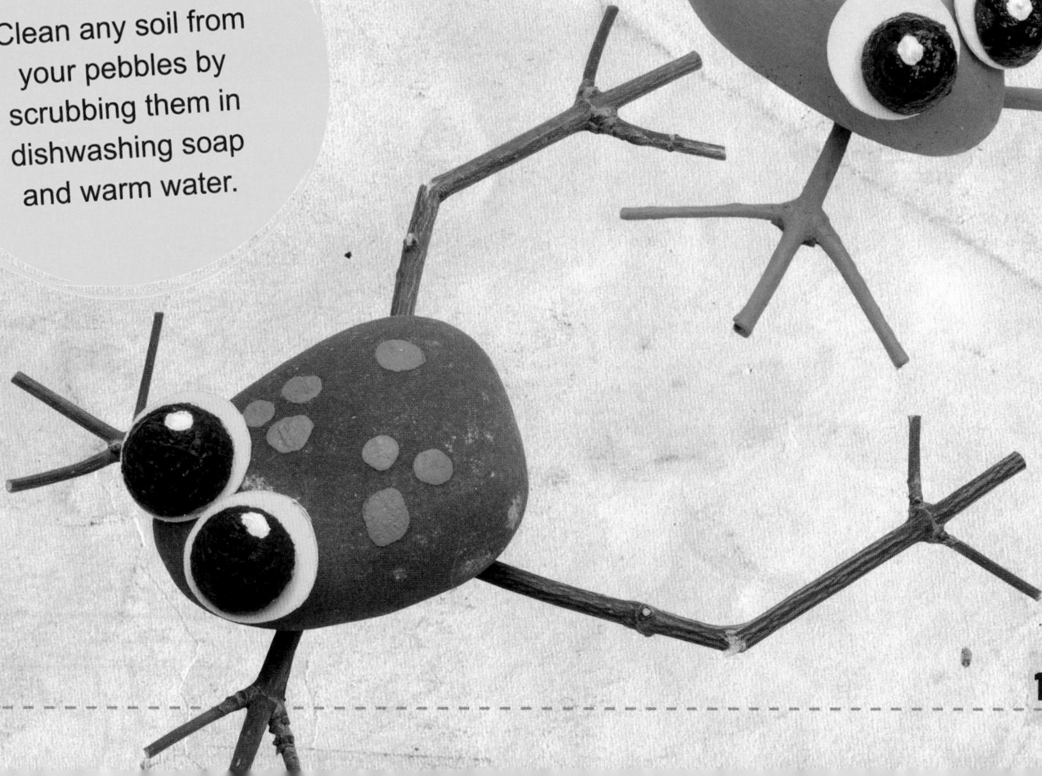

BOING!

Butterflies

Choose clean feathers to make your butterfly wings. Smooth them with your fingers to rejoin any separated parts.

1

Pair up the feathers to make a roughly symmetrical butterfly.

2

Try to use feathers with nice markings. Keep these natural and paint any plainer ones.

3

Cut out two body shapes from cardstock. Paint one of the pieces of cardstock green.

4

Cut off the quill ends from the feathers. Glue a pair of feathers to the unpainted piece of cardstock.

5

Add more feathers until you have a pair of colorful wings.

6

Glue the painted piece of cardstock on top. Use a pen to add some stripes.

7

Paint the insides of two acorn cups white. When they are dry, glue a dried bean or pea in the middle to make a pair of eyes.

8

Cut two short lengths of thin stick. If they are not too brittle, bend the ends over a little. These will be the antennae.

9

Glue the eyes to the front and the antennae to the back of the butterfly head. Add a smile!

FLUTTER

FLUTTER

FLUTTER

Monster

Are there monsters in your bedroom? Scare them off with this happy little monster friend!

1

Cut a row of three bowls from the base of an egg carton.

2

Glue the bowls onto another egg carton to make the monster's body.

3

To make the feet, cut both ends off the lid of an egg carton.

4

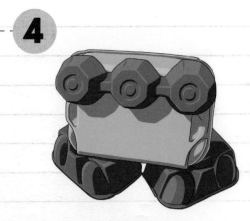

Glue the ends to the base of the monster's body.

5

Cut two pointed parts from the base of an egg carton, for the horns. Paint the monster.

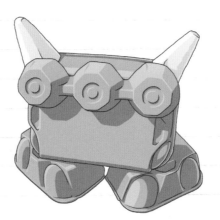

6

Paint on spots and claws, and three circles of pink. Glue googly eyes on top. Add a smile to this not-so-scary monster!

SO CUTE!

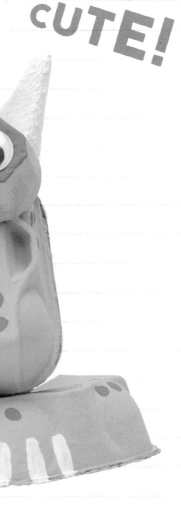

Bee

Get buzzing and make a pretty bumblebee!

You will need

One egg carton

Yellow, black, blue, and white paint

White and blue cardstock

Two yellow bendy straws

Two googly eyes

1

Paint the top of your carton yellow and the bottom black. Add black stripes to the top.

2

At one end of the carton, use a pencil to make two holes. Cut the bendy part off two straws and insert into the holes.

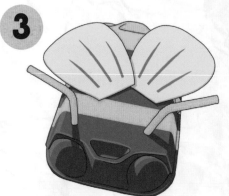

3

Cut out two wings from white cardstock. Paint veins on the wings, then glue into position. Paint a mouth onto your bee.

4

Add blue circles of cardstock behind the eyes to make them stand out. Glue the eyes to the blue circles and then to the egg carton. Buzz, buzz, your bee is ready!

Bracelet

You could make this lovely bracelet for yourself or give it to a friend as a pretty present.

1 Cut three bowls from the base of an egg carton.

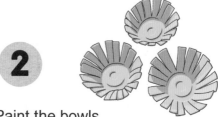

2 Paint the bowls. Cut slits around the edges.

3 Scrunch up some yellow tissue paper and glue it into the center of the bowls.

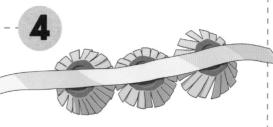

4 Cut a piece of ribbon that is long enough to tie around your wrist. Glue it to the back of the flowers.

5 Your bracelet is ready. Tie it around your wrist and finish with a pretty bow.

Roaring Lion Hand Puppet

Who knew you could make a lion from an egg carton? Your friends will go **WILD** when they see it!

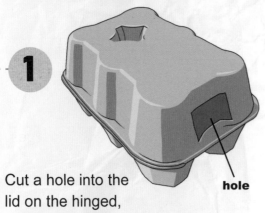

1 Cut a hole into the lid on the hinged, short side of the egg carton. The hole should be big enough to fit two fingers inside.

hole

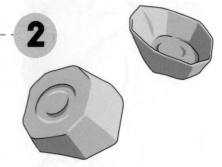

2 Cut two bowls from the base of another egg carton. Trim the sides to give them a sloped edge.

3 Glue the bowls to the top of the first carton. They will be the eyes. Paint the lion's head yellow.

4 Cut slits in a strip of brown felt or cardstock for the mane. You may need two pieces to make a thick mane.

5

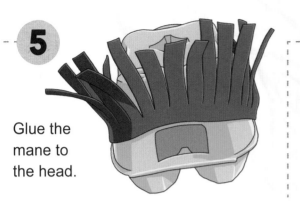

Glue the mane to the head.

6

Cut ears from the white cardstock, paint yellow and glue into position.

7

Add some googly eyes.

8

To make your lion roar, put two fingers in the dip on its head and two fingers in the hole at the back of its head, and your thumb under the carton. Pull up the lid and hear it...

Handy Hint

If you can't find egg cartons with hinges on the short side, cut off the lid of a regular carton and make paper hinges on the short side.

ROAR

Treasure Chest

Nowhere to hide your lovely loot? Problem solved. Make this awesome treasure chest, then hide all your booty in it!

You will need

Three egg cartons
Brown and yellow paint
Yellow cardstock
Ribbon for the treasure

1 Paint an egg carton brown.

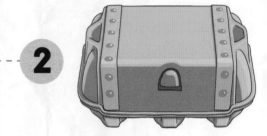

2 Cut two strips of yellow cardstock and glue to the top of the carton. Draw on some rivets with an orange pen.

3 Fold a piece of yellow cardstock in half, and cut out a padlock, as shown.

4 Draw on the keyhole with a black pen.

5

Cut out circles from the bases of two more egg cartons. Glue them to the ribbon to make treasure, and paint yellow.

6

You can make necklaces and gold, too. Keep it hidden from any pirates, though!

Witch

1

Cut two bowls
and one pointed part
from the base of an egg carton.

2

Glue the two
bowls together, to
make a barrel. Paint
all the parts black.

3

Paint a foam ball
yellow. Glue to the
top of the barrel.

4

Cut a strip of
purple felt. Make
slits along one edge.
Glue to the inside of the hat.

5

Cut a cape from some black
felt and glue it to the body.

6

Draw on some
features and make
a pumpkin. You
will need another
barrel, orange
paint, a green
straw, and felt.

138

Cute Noses

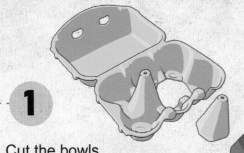

1

Cut the bowls
and the pointed parts
from the base of an egg carton.

2

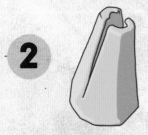

Use a pointed part to make
a beak. Cut a slit in it and
paint yellow.

3

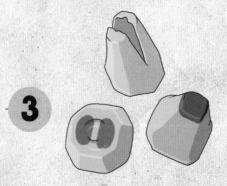

You can make a piglet's nose
from a bowl. Paint it pink and
add some nostrils. A mouse's
nose is made from a pointed
part. Paint it gray, with a black
tip. Add some thin strips of black
cardstock for the whiskers.

4

Make small holes with a
pencil on both sides of each
nose. Tie a length of elastic
string to each nose and they
are ready to wear! Which
one do you like best?

Cute Chicken

This cute chicken is the perfect egg-holder! Make a row of these clucky cuties—they'll brighten up any kitchen.

You will need

One egg carton
White or brown paint
Red and yellow cardstock
Two googly eyes

1

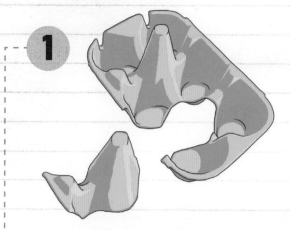

Cut the corner from the base of an egg carton. Paint your chicken white or brown.

2

Fold a small piece of red cardstock in half. Cut out a half-heart shape. You will need to make two of these— one for the chicken's crest and one for its wattle.

3

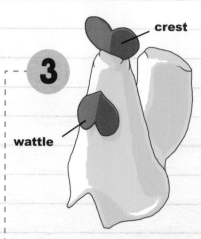

crest

wattle

Glue the crest and wattle to the body, as shown above.

4

Using the same method you used in step 2, cut out a triangular beak.

5

Glue the beak in place. Add some googly eyes.

6

Why not make a row of chickens from one long egg carton? You could keep all your Easter eggs in it!

Fairy Magic

Do you love fairies? You certainly will once you've made this pretty little fairy!

1

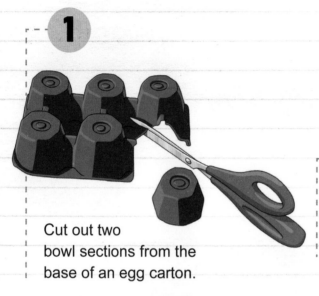

Cut out two bowl sections from the base of an egg carton.

2

Glue the bowls together to make a barrel.

3

Glue on the foam ball. Paint the ball and the bowls. For the hair, glue on some yarn.

4

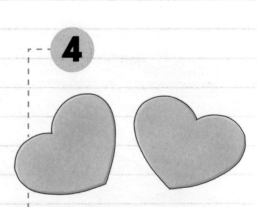

For the wings, cut out two hearts from felt or cardstock.

5

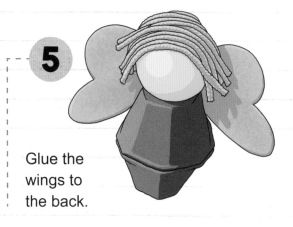

Glue the wings to the back.

6

Draw on some eyes and a friendly smile and your fairy is ready to wave her magic wand!

Handy Hint
Make a few of these magical fairies so you have an entire fairy kingdom.

Fire Engine

Save the day by making this amazing fire engine. You could make two so that you have your very own fire station!

You will need

Two egg cartons

Cardboard

Red, white, blue, and yellow paint

The tops of two toothpaste tubes

Three straws

Shiny corrugated cardstock

1

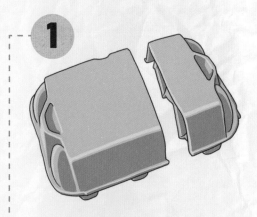

Cut an egg carton in two, as shown. The large section will be the cab.

2

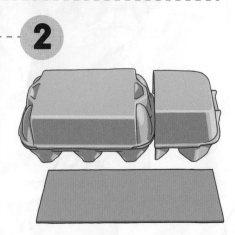

Glue the cab and another egg carton to a piece of cardboard.

3

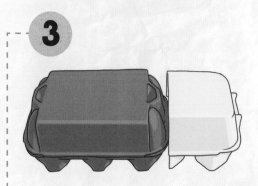

Paint the back section red, and the front part white. When the paint is dry, add some blue windows.

4

Cut out six circles from the thick cardstock for the wheels. Paint and glue in place. Glue two tube tops to the top of the cab.

5

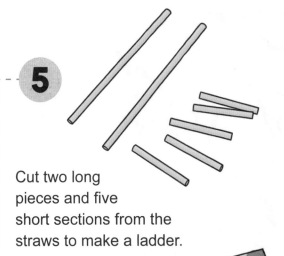

Cut two long pieces and five short sections from the straws to make a ladder.

6

Glue the ladder to the top of the truck.

7

Make a hazard sign from cardboard for the front of the truck, as shown.

8

Glue a piece of shiny corrugated cardstock to the truck's side. Your fire engine is ready to zoom into action!

NEE-NAW NEE-NAW

Christmas Tree

It's Christmastime! Fill your house with festive cheer by making this pretty little tree.

1

Draw a large triangle on a piece of cardboard. Add a pot shape to the bottom. Cut out.

2

Cut 15 bowls from the base of the egg cartons.

3

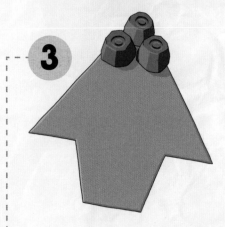

Glue the bowls to the top of the tree, so they fit together snugly.

4

Cover the tree with bowls, but leave the pot section uncovered. Leave to dry.

5

Paint the tree green and paint the pot red.

6

Cut out lots of circles from shiny cardstock, to make hanging balls. Glue them onto your tree.

7

Cut out a star from thick cardstock, and paint it yellow.

8

Glue the star to the top of your tree. Attach a loop of ribbon to the back of the tree, so you can hang it up at Christmastime.

Handy Hint

You can make this tree as large as you like—you just need lots of egg cartons!

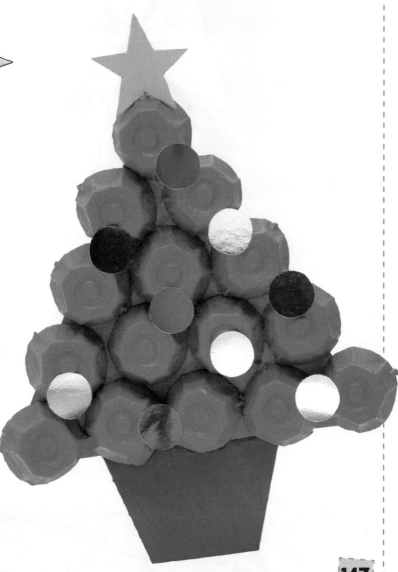

Happy Hippo

You will need

Three egg cartons
Pink and white paint
Cardboard
Two googly eyes

1

Glue two egg cartons onto a piece of cardboard.

2

Cut six bowls from the base of another egg carton.

3

Glue two bowls onto the head to make the hippo's eyes.

4

For the feet, glue the remaining four bowls onto the base. Paint the hippo pink.

5

Add spots, toenails, and googly eyes to the hippo. Paint the inside of the mouth orange and the teeth white. Cut two tusks from the thick cardstock and glue them to the front of the mouth.

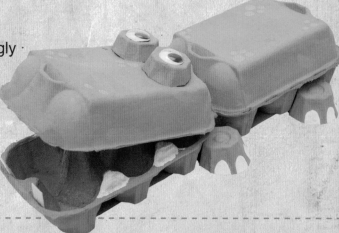

Rocket

5, 4, 3, 2, 1...get ready for blast-off with this bright rocket.

You will need

Three egg cartons
Paint, including red and blue

1

Cut two pointed parts from the base of an egg carton. Paint them red. Paint another egg carton blue.

2

Use a pencil to make two holes in the end of the egg carton. Insert the pointed parts and glue into position.

3

Cut off the corner of another egg carton, to make a triangle.

4

Glue the triangle to the top of the egg carton, and paint blue. Paint on some details, including windows, and your cool rocket is ready to go!

WHOOSH

149

Cute Crab

This cheerful little crab will look cute in a bathroom or with other sea creatures.

You will need

Two egg cartons
Cardstock
Paint
Two metal fasteners
Two googly eyes

1 Cut two bowls from the base of an egg carton.

2 Glue the bowls to the top of another carton, for the eyes.

3 From cardstock, cut two claws. Make sure they are large enough to fit around your crab's body, as shown.

4 Now paint the claws.

5 Paint the crab's body, and add some spots to its shell.

6

Use a pencil to push a hole through the claw and shell of the crab. Attach each claw to the body with a metal fastener.

Make the holes in step 6 smaller than the head of the metal fastener.

Handy Hint

Make the holes in step 6 smaller than the head of the metal fastener.

7

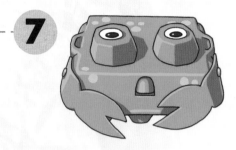

Add some googly eyes. Your crab is now ready, but be careful it doesn't pinch you!

Caterpillar Pencil Holder

You will need

Two egg cartons

Paint, including green

Cardboard

Felt

Two bendy straws

Googly eyes

1 Cut the bowls from the base of an egg carton.

2 Glue two bowls together, to make a barrel. Make six barrels.

3 Paint the barrels bright colors. Cut a strip of cardboard, paint it green, and then glue your barrels onto it.

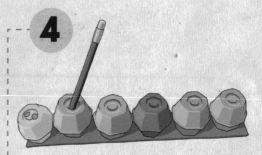

4 Use a pencil to make a hole in the top of five barrels. Leave the end barrel.

5 Make two small holes in the top of the end barrel. Insert two pieces of bendy straw. Glue googly eyes onto circles of felt, and add a smile. Place your pencils in the holes—your pencil holder is ready!

Crocodile

This snappy croc will keep guard outside your bedroom. Why not make another crocodile and let them snap at each other?

You will need

Four egg cartons
(one must have hinges on the short side)
Cardboard
Green and yellow paint
Two googly eyes

1

Cut two bowls from the bottom of an egg carton for the eyes.

2

Cut about five pointed parts from the bottom of another egg carton, for the spiky tail. Cut them into different sizes.

3

Place the short-side opening egg carton upright, with another regular carton next to it, upside-down. Arrange the tail spikes in a line, as shown. Cut a piece of cardboard the same length as the crocodile.

4

Glue all the parts onto the cardboard. Glue the eye pieces to the top of the head.

5

Paint the crocodile a bright green, with yellow spots. Add googly eyes.

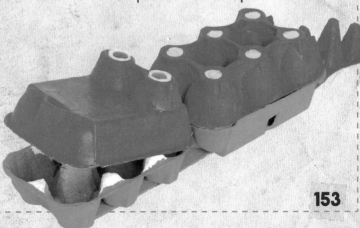

153

Flower Garland

1

Cut the pointed parts from the bottom of an egg carton.

2

Cut a slit in each corner of the pointed parts. Bend the four corners outward.

3

Cut the edges into a petal shape. Paint them and leave to dry. Glue one pointed part onto another to make a flower. Repeat steps 1 to 3 to make as many flowers as you like.

4

Make a small hole in the middle of a flower. Thread through a piece of string.

5

Tie a knot in the string, as shown, then thread on your next flower.

6

Repeat step 5 until you have threaded on all your flowers. Tie a knot under the last flower. Decorate your bedroom with your beautiful flower garland.

Snails

**Blaze a trail with these snails—
all your friends will want one!**

1

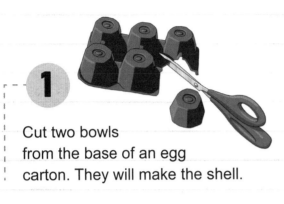

Cut two bowls from the base of an egg carton. They will make the shell.

2

Cut out a long triangle from cardboard. This will be the body. Paint the body and the shell pieces.

3

Glue the shell pieces onto either side of the body. Hold in place with a rubber band until dry.

4

Cut a straw so the bendy part is in the middle. Make a hole in the body with a pencil. Insert the straw and bend upward.

5

Repeat steps 1 to 4 to make another snail. Add spots or stripes to the shell, googly eyes, and a smile. Why not make a set and line them up!

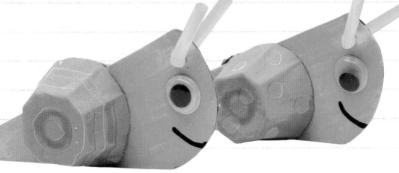

Flower Wreath

This beautiful flower wreath
will brighten up a dull, rainy
day and add some springtime
color to your home.

1

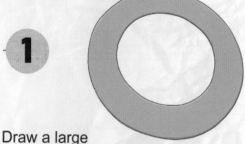

Draw a large
circle onto a piece of
cardboard. Draw a smaller circle
inside. Cut out the large circle.
Use a pencil to make a hole for your
scissors, then cut out the middle
circle to make a ring. Paint it green.

2

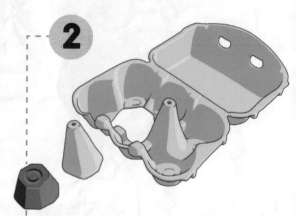

Cut the bowls and pointed
parts from the bottom of
the egg cartons.

3

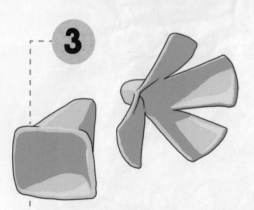

Cut a slit in each corner
of the pointed parts. Bend
the four corners outward.

4

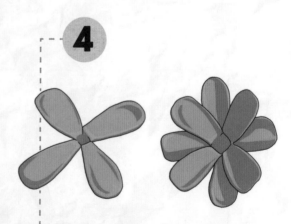

Cut the edges into a petal shape.
Paint them. When they are dry, glue
one pointed part onto another.

156

5

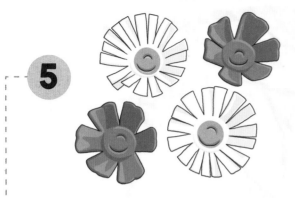

To make other types of flower, cut slits along the sides of the bowls, either close together or far apart, and bend outward. Paint lots of different colors.

6

Cut some leaves from the cardboard and paint them green. When the leaves and flowers are all dry, glue your flowers onto the ring.

7

Scrunch up some small pieces of tissue paper and glue in the centers of the flowers. Glue a piece of ribbon to the back of the garland. Find a spot in your home to hang your flower wreath — why not try one on your bedroom door?

Tugboat

This tugboat is so simple to make, you could make lots of them—and have plenty of time to play with them afterward.

1

Cut the top off a long egg carton, and paint it. Paint a small egg carton a different color.

2

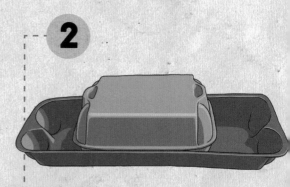

Glue the small egg carton onto the middle of the long carton.

3

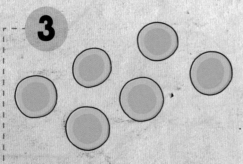

Cut out lots of yellow circles. Paint the centers pale blue. These will be the portholes.

CHUG CHUG

4

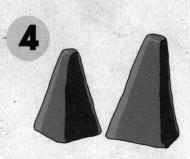

Cut two pointed parts from the base of an egg carton, and paint. These will be the funnels.

5

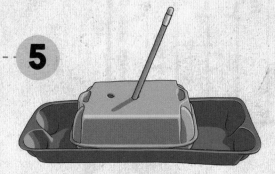

Use a pencil to make two holes along the top of the boat. Insert the funnels and glue into position.

6

Cut out a cloud shape from gray cardstock. Make a slit in the bottom, and slot onto one of funnels, for billowing smoke. Your tugboat is now ready to go to work!

Quarto is the authority on a wide range of topics.
Quarto educates, entertains and enriches the lives of
our readers—enthusiasts and lovers of hands-on living.
www.quartoknows.com

Publisher: Maxime Boucknooghe
Editorial Director: Victoria Garrard
Art Director: Miranda Snow
Editors: Sophie Hallam, Sarah Eason and Jennifer Sanderson
Designer: Paul Myerscough
Photographer: Michael Wicks
Illustrator: Tom Connell
With thanks to our wonderful models Islah, Ethan, and Ania.

© 2019 Quarto Publishing plc

First published in the United States in 2019
by QEB Publishing,
an imprint of The Quarto Group
6 Orchard Road, Suite 100
Lake Forest, CA 92630
T: +1 949 380 7510
F: +1 949 380 7575
www.QuartoKnows.com

A CIP record for this book is available from the Library of Congress.

ISBN 978 1 78603 979 8

Manufactured in Guangdong, China CC072020

9 8 7 6 5 4 3 2